How to Create a Better Future by Building
Your Courage, Capacity, and Wisdom

Choosing
Leadership

REVISED
and
EXPANDED

DR. LINDA GINZEL

Health Communications, Inc.
Boca Raton, Florida

www.hcibooks.com

Library of Congress Cataloging-in-Publication Data
is available through the Library of Congress

© 2022 WiserYounger Inc.

ISBN-13: 978-07573-2437-6 (Paperback)
ISBN-10: 07573-2437-1 (Paperback)
ISBN-13: 978-07573-2438-3 (ePub)
ISBN-10: 07573-2438-X (ePub)

Publisher: Health Communications, Inc.
      301 Crawford Blvd., Suite 200
      Boca Raton, FL 33432-3762

Author photo © Tomer Keyser.
Cover, interior design and formatting by Larissa Hise Henoch

To Boaz Keysar,
the best choice
I ever made.

Leadership and learning are indispensable to each other.

CONTENTS

FOREWORD BY DANIEL GILBERT ix

HOW TO USE THE REVISED AND EXPANDED EDITION xi

INTRODUCTION: LEADERSHIP IS A CHOICE 1

PART I: THE WORKBOOK   9

CHAPTER 1: Writing Your Earliest Leadership Story   11

CHAPTER 2: Defining Leading and Managing   27

CHAPTER 3: Understanding Gist: The Core Essence   45

CHAPTER 4: Learning from the Experience of Others   69

CHAPTER 5: Learning from Our Own Experience   93

CHAPTER 6: Being Wiser, Younger   109

CHAPTER 7: Developing Leadership Skills Every Day   125

PART II: LEADERSHIP MODULES   143

Introduction (A–C)   145

Chapter 1 (1.A–1.D)   151

Chapter 2 (2.A–2.C)   161

Chapter 3 (3.A–3.C)   167

Chapter 4 (4.A–4.D)   171

Chapter 5 (5.A–5.B)   181

Chapter 6 (6.A–6.C)   183

Chapter 7 (7.A–7.C)   191

ACKNOWLEDGMENTS: REVISED AND EXPANDED EDITION   197
ACKNOWLEDGMENTS: FIRST EDITION   201
APPENDIX A: ACTIVITY INDEX   205
APPENDIX B: LEADERSHIP MODULE INDEX   207
APPENDIX C: VIDEO INDEX   209
CITATIONS   211
INDEX   219
ABOUT THE AUTHOR   231

Illustrations

FIGURES

Figure 2.1: Effective Followers   40
Figure 3.1: Reversible Figure   55
Figure 7.1: Average Leadership Capacity   126
Figure 7.2: Be Wiser, Younger   127

TABLES

Table 2.1: Leadership and Management   29
Table 4.1: SPA Vicarious-Learning Framework   74
Table 4.2: Jonathan Eig's Interview Advice   76
Table 6.1: Preparation Worksheet   121

FOREWORD

When a gosling hatches, it immediately looks around until it locates a bright moving object, and then it instinctively follows that object wherever it goes. The object is typically the gosling's mother, so this works out nicely for everyone.

Following is the most natural thing on earth, which is why even a minute-old bird can do it. Leading, on the other hand, takes work. But what kind of work does it take? Does it take knowledge or practice? Does it take a week or a lifetime? Can anybody do it? How about me?

No one knows the answers to these questions better than Linda Ginzel, who has spent her life teaching people how to stop waddling behind the gaggle and start flying in front of the skein. Linda was trained as an experimental psychologist, but after receiving her PhD from Princeton University, she decided she wanted to work in a laboratory that was roughly the size of the world, and so she began teaching in business schools—first Stanford, then Northwestern, and then finally the University of Chicago, where for more than twenty-five years she has been an award-winning professor whose students have gone on to become successful leaders in many of the world's top corporations and organizations.

When she isn't busy educating her students, Linda keeps busy educating the rest of us. In addition to being a pioneer and innovator in the teaching of leadership, Linda is one of the country's leading consumer advocates whose work on product safety has saved thousands of lives. President Clinton personally presented her with the President's Volunteer Service Award, the nation's highest honor for volunteer service directed at solving critical social problems, and she has served on President Obama's transition team, testified before the United States Congress, and appeared on national television shows ranging from the *Today Show* to *Oprah*.

All of which is simply to say that Linda knows a whole lot about leadership—about what it is, and more importantly, what it isn't. One of the things she knows is that leaders don't lead by lecturing, but by acting. And so rather than writing a textbook that tells you how to become a leader, she has written a workbook that *shows* you. *Choosing Leadership* doesn't ask you to read it—it asks you to participate in it. If you want to sit still while some self-appointed guru explains how you can become the leader of your very own company, country, or religion in three easy steps, then you've come to the wrong place. But if you want to go on a journey with a wise and inspiring guide, a scientist and teacher who has been the personal navigator for thousands of successful leaders over a quarter of a century, then there is no other place to be.

So look around. Linda Ginzel is your bright moving object. Go where she takes you. You'll never be the same old bird again.

—DANIEL GILBERT
Edgar Pierce Professor of Psychology,
Harvard University
Author of Stumbling on Happiness

HOW TO USE
THE REVISED AND
EXPANDED EDITION

Welcome to the revised and expanded edition of *Choosing Leadership*. First, let me share the history. The original workbook was born out of handouts, exercises, and activities to complement a capstone leadership course I created at the University of Chicago's Booth School of Business. Students were better able to understand my philosophy, from the context of the terms I used to the importance of crafting one's own personal definition of leadership. Word spread, and before long people beyond my classroom asked for copies of my course handouts, not only for themselves but for their coworkers, friends, and children.

I was gratified and humbled when the workbook that evolved from those materials became a bestseller. This revised and expanded edition now includes Leadership Modules that guide the reader in how to use the book to teach and learn together with a group. They include links to online instructional videos and they also provide step-by-step guidance to create group experiences designed to enable reflection, explore ideas, and enhance self-understanding. These group experiences create collective wisdom and encourage learners to make better and more thoughtful choices. Through individual written reflection and peer discussions, readers learn how to coach themselves and others while gaining self-understanding and confidence.

The original edition of *Choosing Leadership* was used by a diverse group of people implementing its lessons across a wide range of personal and professional contexts. Many of them have graciously offered me their feedback, told me how they used the workbook for their purposes, and modeled how others can tailor the material for their program's needs. The contributors work in both academia and the business world and have used the book with high school athletes, undergraduate and graduate students, medical residents, and a faith-based group. They even started a book club. The applications, as these contributors have shown, are only limited by one's imagination.

Below is a list of these contributors, followed by their testimonials and descriptions, in their own words, about how they used *Choosing Leadership*. Let their ideas be a springboard for you as you gain a deeper understanding of the true meaning of leadership—and learn more about yourself, your vision for the future, and how to impart this vision to others.

1. Char Bennington, human resources director of employee development. *Staff meet in small, cross-functional discussion groups.*

2. Marjorie Bentley, college director of admissions. *Rural high school students attend a college preparatory summer program.*

3. Bill Henderson, law school professor. *Teams of law school students teach their peers.*

4. Beck Jurasius, college student. *High school athletes learn about individual and team effectiveness.*

5. Jasmine Kwong, MBA student. *Created the book club group, "Friends with Green Pens."*

6. Kimberly Reiser, high school teacher. *Leadership education in high school business and marketing courses.*

7. Rick Riddering, director of leadership development. *Teaches adult learning at a small, Christian liberal arts college.*

8. Dr. Joon Shim, program director of general surgery residency. *Surgical residents discuss leadership in a longitudinal workshop.*

9. Grace Soetikno Pandji, director of international business. *Training of employees for one of the largest pharmaceutical companies in Indonesia.*

Char Bennington, Director, Employee Development, Human Resources, The University of Chicago, Booth School of Business

As a valuable addition to our Leadership Development program here at Chicago Booth, our work with the *Choosing Leadership* book has been amazing. Compared to other leadership development opportunities, the book is not only incredibly inexpensive, it is also very effective. We have formed twenty-plus small discussion groups of staff members who meet usually monthly to work through and discuss the concepts in the chapters and the many exercises. An added benefit is that the groups are all cross-functional, so participants meet other colleagues across the organization.

Participants benefit from engaging with the *Choosing Leadership* book in so many ways. Each exercise expands their thinking about leadership in a different way as they reflect on their own experiences, creating their own definition as to what being a "leader" means. By working through the exercises, participants discover the many ways they have already demonstrated many leadership behaviors. The readings, exercises, and discussions change how they see themselves and give participants the opportunity to build upon behaviors and skills they already have. Participants also get to test new behaviors and skills and make choices as to the kind of leader they want to be.

Due to the many benefits to staff members and the organization and the ease with which we can implement the program, bringing our staff members together to discuss and be impacted by *Choosing Leadership* will be an ongoing part of our efforts to develop leaders within Booth.

Marjorie Bentley, Senior Associate Director of Admissions, Trott Director of the Emerging Rural Leaders Program, The University of Chicago

Linda Ginzel's *Choosing Leadership* has been the cornerstone of our Emerging Rural Leaders curriculum since the creation of the program in 2019. The Emerging Rural Leaders program is designed to support students from rural and small-town high schools across the United States in their college search process by introducing them to a residential college experience and connecting them with a network of talented and engaged peers. While I'm sure that the book is a fantastic tool for business executives, we have used *Choosing Leadership* with students at every point in their high school career, including freshmen, and couldn't recommend it more for high schoolers!

I have seen Linda's book give hundreds of fourteen- and fifteen-year-olds the concepts and tools that they need to think critically about their life experiences and goals for their future. I am always blown away by the amount of thoughtful self-reflection that these students are eager to engage in when given the right tools. There is clearly a hunger from our high schoolers to figure out how to think critically and be "wiser, younger," and Linda shows them that they can through the exercises in the book!

Having a physical book (and a green pen, of course!) for students struggling to navigate such a virtual world has also been a game changer for our students these past few years. They can walk away from our programs with a tangible reminder of their time together, written responses to track their growth over time, and a reservoir of exercises and ideas that they can revisit over the course of their high school careers.

I truly believe that *Choosing Leadership* is an invaluable resource for anyone, no matter their age, but I am especially grateful to have a book that has galvanized and guided this current generation of young leaders.

Professor William Henderson, Indiana University School of Law, Bloomington,

Deliberative Leadership required course materials:
- *Linda Ginzel, PhD,* Choosing Leadership
- *Additional materials posted on Canvas and/or distributed in paper copy in class*

The core of this course is built around *Choosing Leadership* (2018) by Linda Ginzel, PhD. I adopted this book because so many of its exercises (called "Activities" in the book) are consistent with many of the best Deliberative Leadership classes over the last four years. In addition, Professor Ginzel is a distinguished social psychologist who has pioneered new ways to more effectively teach leadership at several top business schools. Based on feedback from prior years, I believe most students will appreciate the structure of this expertly designed book, particularly if combined with ample latitude for student teams to decide how class time gets allocated. We will complete the first six chapters before spring break. Chapter 7 (the last chapter) is the basis for our capstone assignment.

Weeks two and three include book assignments plus some additional assigned material to build out some of the week's core themes. For weeks four, five, seven, and eight, the team running the class can supplement the book assignment and is free to utilize class time as it sees fit—focus on assigned portions of the book the team finds most interesting or valuable; experiment with supplemental reading, videos, and podcasts that build out the class themes; some combination of these approaches; or something entirely different. I will make myself available to assist students in the planning process, but you are not required to consult with me. In constructing the class, please keep only one principle in mind: maximize the value of the class for your peers.

Beck Jurasius, Student, Stanford University

Beck Jurasius is a junior at Stanford University who majors in mechanical engineering and plays on the men's water polo team. A competitive swimmer with a passion for personal development, Beck created a curriculum for high school athletes with content adapted from Choosing Leadership. *The activities can be integrated into coaching sessions or stand as their own workshops, specifically designed to appeal directly to high school athletes to increase not only their own personal effectiveness but also the effectiveness of their teammates.*

When I was a ten-year-old budding athlete, Professor Ginzel gave me a poster of Michael Phelps titled "Determination." I still have that poster on my wall ten years later because it reminds me of my leadership journey. It was during this time working with different coaches and teachers that I started to ask myself questions about my goals as a student and athlete. My journey was facilitated by Professor Ginzel, who sent me some meaningful books from her leadership journey. From *The Little Prince,* I learned it is important to explore because personal growth occurs outside your comfort zone, and I learned the value of asking good questions. *The Alchemist* helped me to understand the importance of self-determination, perseverance, believing in yourself, and seeing obstacles as a challenge that will help you grow. Professor Ginzel's book *Choosing Leadership* provides all these great lessons for understanding your leadership journey in one ultimate guide. Through relatable examples, challenging questions, engaging exercises, and activities, it provides a personalized path to leadership by reflecting on your own experiences. It is a transformative guide to understanding who you are and who you are as a leader. I say *transformative* because how you choose to lead will change over time with your discovery of self and reflection on your interactions with others. The writing exercises in the book are essential because you will look back on these and keep editing and editing as you have more experiences and refine your leadership definition.

Professor Ginzel's *Choosing Leadership* guides the reader through this process of self-discovery. Through understanding yourself as a leader, you build genuine confidence to become the leader that you want to be. Her work is so impactful that I asked permission to adapt her book to create lessons in leadership for youth athletes. Starting with their definition of leadership and discussing myths about leadership helps all team members realize that in any situation they can lead and that their definition and concept of leadership will grow over time. Through the exercises in the book, the athletes reflect on their experiences that shaped their leadership definition and can identify behaviors that increase their leadership effectiveness. Leadership is different for everyone, and it is about developing your own point of view. Anyone can lead if they choose to. The students in the module began a journey of understanding themselves and creating their own gist by sharing their stories of leadership as well as what leadership means to them. Engaging in these exercises had a visibly positive effect on their confidence and interactions with others. Students can apply the lessons immediately and see results. They go from strength to strength, continuing to build confidence throughout the journey. The program was so successful with athletes that I have now adapted the lessons from Professor Ginzel's book for working with high school students to help them gain confidence in themselves as leaders. There is much to be learned from your own experiences, good and bad, and through reflection you can take charge of your own personal growth and create the path you want for your future. Professor Ginzel's *Choosing Leadership* is the ultimate tour guide for a lifelong learning journey.

Jasmine Kwong, MBA, Associate Director, Center for Decision Research Labs and Programs, The University of Chicago Booth School of Business, Friends with Green Pens

Participants: Jasmine Kwong, MBA16; Wilson Sun, MBA17; Ashwin Avasarala, MBA18; Yiqing (Liz) Dong, MBA18; Akkaravuth (March) Kopsombut, MBA18

Wilson and I are both from Hong Kong, graduates of Booth's part-time MBA program, and huge fans of Linda. In February 2019, we invited a few fellow alumni to form a small group to go through *Choosing Leadership* together so that we could help each other extract more lessons and perspective from the activities. Of course, it also helps to have friends to keep each other accountable and make the experience more fun.

I had never thought of joining a book club before, but here I was co-starting one. We created a group chat to facilitate communications and named ourselves "Friends with Green Pens." We aimed to meet once a month, going through one chapter each time. At our first get-together, we even all wore green. It was wonderful to gather as a group to exchange thoughts and stories, learn from each other's experiences, and grow together. What's better than becoming wiser, younger? Doing so with good company.

Kimberly Reiser, Business Services Pathway Lead, Cherry Creek Innovation Campus Cherry Creek Schools

In the spring of 2019, I was gifted a copy of *Choosing Leadership* by Linda Ginzel. This gift, a book with an accompanying green pen, helped me to develop a leadership curriculum for all students. I have used this book to design and revolutionize courses in business and marketing, creating a new educational experience for students on our new career and technical campus. While traditional high school leadership classes are made of popular students, athletes, and individuals who have already proven they leaders, those students are elected to help with homecoming, prom, dances, hall decorating contests, and making the students' voices heard by the administration. In most cases, these students didn't choose leadership, it chose them. As such, *Choosing Leadership* was a necessary ingredient to add to our leadership courses.

The cover of *Choosing Leadership* tells the reader that they can create a better future for themselves by building their courage, capacity, and wisdom. I have found that to be true for myself and for my students. The book shares insight on the choices we all make every day on being a better person and making the choice to be a leader. My students have been provided opportunities to share their earliest leadership memories, and many

How to Use the Revised and Expanded Edition

of those opportunities have nothing to do with sports or a title that they were given. The students genuinely reflect on their previous behaviors and the lessons they learned, even at a young age. The students in my learning lab are encouraged to write and reflect on a variety of things; two very powerful assignments include "This I Believe" and the "Commencement Speech." These two writing pieces differ because one is focused on what the student believes to be true based on their life experiences, and the commencement speech is for others. The commencement speech is an opportunity to share advice and memories of your time in high school with your entire class. Not everyone gets to deliver a commencement speech to their entire class at a graduation ceremony; however, the memories of just one student may not capture the experiences of the entire class and students may miss out on some valuable advice. The commencement speech can fill a student with hope for their future and the future of others.

Linda shares several nuggets of information throughout the book. Here are a few of my favorites:

- **Leading and managing—the same person both manages and leads.** When you manage, you are in the present. Once in a while you make a choice to create a better future—big or small choices, that is leadership. One is no less important than the other.

- **Experience is a dear teacher, and those around us may not always have the answers.** Leadership development requires asking some tough questions of yourself.

- **If you don't write it down, it doesn't exist.** This is one of my favorites because if you sit next to me in a staff meeting or training, I am constantly writing. Linda encourages those who choose leadership to find a framework that can be easily adaptable to a variety of situations so that you can learn from what you hear and see all around you. The learning takes place because it is a reference for the future, and the mere act of writing it down solidifies your practice.

- **Wiser, younger—you will never be younger than you are today.** What do you want to do next? Why aren't you doing it now?

I had the privilege of introducing Linda to one of my classes last year, and she was wonderful. The stories that she shares, the intention that she uses in life, and of course, the hope she has for the future students who choose leadership is admirable. I am honored to write this on behalf of Linda but also to the book that continues to change the shape of future leaders.

Rick Riddering, Director of Leadership Development, Director of Community Life, Faith Church, Central Staff and Cedar Lake Campus

I teach the course "Leadership" to adult learners completing their degree at Trinity Christian College, a small, Christian liberal arts institution located in the suburbs of Chicago. In addition, I serve as Director of Leadership Development at Faith Church, which is a large church with four locations in northwest Indiana and one in southern Illinois.

Dr. Ginzel's book *Choosing Leadership* is a practical guide that supports my teaching style but most importantly enhances each learner's experience and development. My approach to teaching is not as theoretical as some professors might be when it comes to teaching the topic of leadership. Being that I teach primarily adult learners, I incorporate more of a training format, fully utilizing adult learning theory, which allows me to present a topic that utilizes the experience of the students too. After checking understanding of any given topic, I then encourage and motivate learners to explore ways for them to apply what they've learned to put the theories and new knowledge into practice as soon as possible. I find this to be much more useful with students studying leadership than simply requiring them to memorize and regurgitate terms, definitions, and theories. I'm convinced that new learnings are worthless in the overall leadership development unless a learner has a full understanding of how they apply them to their very own leadership style. Having taught many adult learners throughout my career as a faculty member and a human resource development practitioner, this has served my learners well, and I've come to understand that adult learners especially love this way of teaching. And adult college students are no exception.

Choosing Leadership helped me structure my course to make it much more meaningful for the learner because this book helps to accelerate my students' ability to put leadership theory into practice rooted in their very own giftedness or experience levels. It also helps me to better customize the learning experience for my students because the book's exercises help them to better understand who they are and where they've come from, while at the same time helping them to cast a clearer vision for who they'd like to become as a leader. Students in my courses have often remarked about how much they enjoy the reflective work they've been empowered to do because of Dr. Ginzel's book. They've told me that it's a freeing experience when they finally realize who they truly are, how their personality and experiences have gotten them there, and where they feel they are headed in their overall development as a leader. It's for all these reasons that I strongly endorse *Choosing Leadership* for adult learners in a college classroom or in a corporate conference room.

Joon K. Shim, MD, MPH, FACS, Program Director, General Surgery Residency, Assistant Clinical Professor of Surgery at Columbia University, Vice Chair for the Association for Surgical Education

Choosing Leadership is hope for a better future. There is no formal training in leadership for residents in surgical training. I have been able to address this gap by using *Choosing Leadership,* Professor Ginzel's book, which allows for reflective practice. Voluntary and application based, twenty-one residents were chosen to participate in a longitudinal workshop using Professor Ginzel's book over the last three years. With their busy training schedule, surgical residents have dedicated several months to meet and discuss core values of leadership, committing themselves to change stereotypes about leading and managing and biases in surgery. Group discussions have rejuvenated their sense of meaning in the hospital environment.

Choosing Leadership allows surgeons to normalize conversations about challenges encountered in the course of delivering surgical care to vulnerable patients. These discussions lend themselves to demonstrate the surgical residents, commitment to themselves with self-care and well-being.

Building communication skills with psychological safety, our surgical residents are able to effectively tackle personal and professional challenges with self-awareness, moving toward clarifying their present and future goals. Using Professor Ginzel's book, surgeons are able to identify and address personal challenges and consciously improve and integrate the many facets of their lives as residents in surgical training.

They are ready to define their own success and make choices, respond to their environment, and create the life they desire.

Grace Soetikno Pandji, Director of International Business, Dexa Medica, one of Indonesia's largest pharmaceutical companies

The Leadership Capital class in my AXP-19 EMBA program was an especially important part of my learning journey. It enabled me to embrace a philosophy of courage, capacity, and wisdom that I also wanted to instill in our company's workforce. Despite my obvious limitations of being neither a professor, trainer, nor a facilitator, I was able to initiate changes to transform our leadership fundamentals and culture.

I have found *Choosing Leadership* to be a fountain of wisdom that enhances leadership capabilities and performance for those who invest in it. Each chapter has its own wonderful concepts that are easily explained, which can then be accepted, understood by, and applied to the participants' activities. I used the book to further develop and enhance our company's leadership development programs. To be effective, we made use of a video series summarizing each chapter to emphasize concepts from the book and to facilitate rigorous pre-session or post-session work.

This use has allowed some of our current and future leaders to begin to apply the concepts in the book to real-life work and personal situations. Participants, from directors up to supervisory levels, have been encouraged to keep learning with their team members. They are also mandated to compile a 100-day action plan to apply the new learnings to, and make changes within, their respective domains. The participants were also required to ask questions that would all be answered individually. All the participants were so satisfied with the new concepts of *Choosing Leadership* once it is stated that everyone can be a champion.

As Kurt Lewin said, "There is nothing as practical as a good theory."

Increasing our leadership capacity is a multiplying force because individuals' growth and improvement only beget further improvement. I am passionate about enabling and nurturing this development, not only for the strategic benefits, but also as my contribution to my father's legacy as the founder of the company.

It has been a fulfilling experience to see many of our leaders live out the theories of *Choosing Leadership.* I am extremely grateful for the impact that this book and Professor Ginzel have had on me and the leaders in our company.

Thank you, Professor Linda Ginzel, for your unwavering commitment to leadership.

INTRODUCTION: LEADERSHIP IS A CHOICE

This is a simple statement and the premise of everything that follows: leadership is a choice. If you want to stop reading, you can stop now because you now know the gist of this book: You make a choice to lead.

However, leadership is *your* choice. You make choices that will change the future, create better outcomes, generate more meaning, and help shape your future self. On what basis do you make your choices? This book is, in large part, about answering that question as part of working on your future self. The self is a work in progress. It doesn't matter how old you are, what your job is, or whether you have an official-sounding title. We all have hopes for our future self.

This book is your companion on the lifelong journey to be wiser, younger.

For group learning, use Leadership Module A: Building Community (40 Minutes)

Here's a story from Ivan, one of my former students, who tells how his choices transformed him from "a chubby boy who was shy to ask for directions on the street to a person who was in charge of himself and was now ready to choose to lead other people."

One of my early leadership experiences happened when I came to study in the United States at the age of seventeen from a small regional city in Russia. I had to start making my own choices, choosing my own behavior, and making my own living. I started to exercise regularly, lost weight, studied hard to get good marks, worked on a part-time job, and joined the Corps of Cadets.

I think leadership starts when you choose to take ownership and responsibility of your own actions. You can't lead other people if you don't know how to lead yourself. When I came to the US at seventeen, it was the first time that I truly had to take the lead of myself.

Throughout this book, you will read a variety of "early leadership stories" such as Ivan's story. Taken together, these stories illustrate that each of us has many more opportunities, and varieties of choice, than we recognize. We all tend to operate on default mode based on behaviors that have become habits. If you are successful and capable, you probably have pretty good habits. If you were never to have picked up this book, you would probably do just fine in life by operating on your defaults. But you can create better habits by recognizing, changing, and improving those defaults. Let's start with a few definitions. Throughout these pages, I often use the word *champion* because this book is not intended exclusively for business executives. You might think I'm writing for people in the C-suite—and I believe this topic will interest them—but everyone can be a champion. A champion is someone who advocates for something they care about. This book will be your companion on your journey to become a better champion for yourself, your family, and your friends—at home, in the workplace, and in the community.

Another definition I want to clarify early on is *leadership*. When we use the word leadership, people get caught up in what they think it should mean and often get it mixed up with *management*. Harvard's John Kotter has said that managers promote stability while leaders press for change. This implies that some people are managers and others are leaders. I see it differently: The same person both manages *and* leads.

When you are managing, you are in the present. You may be managing a budget, meeting expectations, checking inventory, or making sure you've got diapers in the house. Whatever it is you're doing that's for the present is management, and it's very important. Most of the time, you're managing.

Every once in a while, you make a choice to create a better future. This can be a small or a big choice, but either way, this is leadership. At this point, when you decide to change the present to create a different future, you are making the choice to lead. This is my definition of leadership: behavioral choices we make in order to create a better future.

In doing so, you will be wiser, younger. You will never be younger than you are today, but you can be wiser. Much of the work we do in this book will help you to become that wiser self sooner rather than later.

Here are a few more important things to consider: My watchword for champions is *choice*. It's important to avoid getting caught up in labels when choosing whether to manage or lead. Managing is no less important than leading.

But don't simply accept definitions as they are presented. Using this book, you will form your own definitions based on your personal experiences and unique perspectives. Our definitions—and whether they are articulated, written down, and understood—affect our behavior. You may currently use a definition of leadership that involves a lot of myths, some of which may hold that you have to be tall, extroverted, attractive, and older in order to lead. Like many people, you may think that leaders must have a big title, a corner office, or credentials from a fancy school. If you have bought into these myths, now is the time to rethink them. They limit your choices.

Instead of thinking about people who are "leaders," think of the choices these people made to lead. As a champion, according to my use of the term, you have an opportunity on any given day to both manage and to lead. How do you want to embody the role of a champion? The choice is yours.

Every day of your life, you have an opportunity to lead.

To lead and to manage. Some years ago, Duke University's Richard Larrick challenged me to talk about leadership as a behavior as opposed to something done by a person or a position. I have found his challenge to be difficult and enlightening. Join me in following his lead, and in everyday conversation, do your best to stop using the nouns "leader" and "manager." Instead, try using the infinitives "to lead" and "to manage."

This is why I call this book *Choosing Leadership.*

That choice can be difficult for many reasons. When we don't understand something, perhaps due to anxiety or even fear, we look to others for answers. Many of us look to exemplars, such as bosses or teachers. But they don't have all the answers. Leadership development requires asking some tough questions of yourself. This is difficult to do. So to truly grow, you have to be at a point in your life where you want to ask yourself these questions and have the maturity to face the answers.

There are many books about leadership, so there is plenty to read on this topic. But at some point, you have to do the work of self-development you need in order to lead. No one else can do this work for you, but this book can serve as your guide.

Steve Jobs once said, "Your time is limited, so don't waste it living someone else's life." That's a good quote to accompany you on this journey. This is your life. If you don't know yourself well enough to make choices based on what you value, it's easier to let other people make choices for you. For many of us, this is quite sustainable and even fulfilling—until it's not. One day, you may look at yourself and ask, *Why am I doing this? What does it all mean?* We don't have to wait for such a crisis of identity to bring us to these questions.

Experience is a dear teacher.
—BENJAMIN FRANKLIN

Each chapter offers a variety of activities intended to help you reflect on the data from your life. The activities require you to write things down, things that may have only been in your mind until this point. There is something magical about writing. Once you write something down, it becomes observable, something you can revisit, show to others, collect, edit, and expand upon. In other words, it becomes data. You can't collect or write down everything, so you have to be selective about what you want to record. But writing is key. If you write something down, you might do nothing with it. But if you don't write it down, it will likely disappear from your mind. And you won't be able to use it for changing your behavior and improving your future outcomes. The activities presented in this book serve as vehicles for you to make concrete your own understandings of life's lessons.

 "Verba volant, scripta manent" is a Latin proverb. Literally translated, it means "spoken words fly away, written words remain."

In addition to activities, *Choosing Leadership, Revised and Expanded,* has Leadership Modules for each chapter. These modules provide step-by-step guidance to create group experiences designed to enable reflection, explore ideas, and enhance self-understanding. Participating in group experiences creates collective wisdom and encourages you to make better and more thoughtful choices. Through peer discussions, you learn how to become your own coach. While gaining self-understanding, you'll also gain confidence. You will realize that you know how to lead and be wiser, younger.

For group learning, use Leadership Module B: Beginnings and Endings (15 Minutes)

Why I Wrote This Book

Before getting started on yourself, you may want some background on me. Here's a bit about how I ended up being dragged kicking and screaming into the study of leadership and why I wrote this book.

I'm an experimental social psychologist, and every day I help executives put psychology into practice. I am the last person on earth who thought I'd be writing a book on leadership. My first love was management. In 1986, I was a doctoral student at Princeton University. I took a leave of absence and worked for Mutual of New York as a corporate training consultant in designing educational programs, and that's where I discovered my interest in management.

My first faculty job was at Stanford Business School. I was the first Princeton PhD in psychology to take a job in a business school, and back in 1989, that was considered heretical. I eventually taught management to MBA students at Stanford, Northwestern's Kellogg School of Business, and the University of Chicago's Booth School of Business and found I was able to help students put knowledge of social psychology to use on a daily basis. Teaching for me is about more than pouring knowledge into student's heads; it is about conveying what they are capable of doing with that knowledge.

In 2005, a friend and Booth colleague, Howard Haas, asked me to teach his long-standing leadership course. In his professional career, he had worked his way up from sales manager to CEO of Sealy, the mattress company, then had spent twenty years reinventing himself as a teaching CEO. I remember him saying, "Linda, I'm going to retire at some point, and I'd like you take over my leadership class." I proposed we co-teach his course so that I could learn from him but also contribute my own ideas. Over time, I developed an appreciation for how difficult it is to teach and learn leadership. There is no consensus as to what "leadership" is. And it isn't like social psychology or any other academic field where training in the discipline is deep and narrow. Leadership is broad and wide because it is multidisciplinary. There is no leadership canon. Because of this, there is no explicit body of literature that you can read, knowing that when you are finished studying you will be recognized as an expert in the field.

Leadership is also a multibillion-dollar industry where people will sell you anything you are willing to buy. (If you want to read more about this, Stanford's Jeffrey Pfeffer has an eye-opening book called *Leadership*

BS.) But in everything that I've read about leadership, I've never found a framework about it that I was happy to adopt and live by. I had to create my own way of thinking. I call this framework *leadership capital,* paying homage to the late Gary S. Becker's theory of human capital. The intangible assets of leadership capital are found in my definition: the wisdom to decide when to manage and when to lead, together with the courage and capacity to act on your choices. I don't know if I can help you to be a better consumer of leadership products, but I do believe this book can help you think in more complex ways about the value of the intangible leadership assets already within you.

Wrestling with leadership ideas inspired me to write this book. It stems from something I created for one of my Booth MBA leadership courses so that my students could continue to build their leadership capital outside my classroom. I only have my students' attention for a limited amount of time, but they have the remainder of their lives to continue their leadership development. The same is true for you.

This book is your companion. On its pages, you will have the opportunity to process your own lessons, reflect on your experiences, and ultimately transform your behavior. I hope this book will help you create a better future. The world around us changes by the second. Leadership is many things, but it's not a target, or something that can be figured out, or wielded only when a situation demands. It's a skill that needs to be constantly practiced and developed. This book will teach you the skills of leadership, then help you keep that knowledge active so that you can continue learning every day of your life. In the end, you are the only person capable of steering this process, applying knowledge, and changing your behavior. But this book can get you started on a path—your own path. Enjoy the journey!

> ## If you don't write it down, it doesn't exist.
> —LINDA GINZEL IN RICHARD THALER'S *MISBEHAVING*

For group learning, use Leadership Module C: Choosing Leadership Introduction (15 Minutes)

PART 1

The Workbook

CHAPTER 1

Writing Your Earliest Leadership Story

This recipe calls for leadership.

—KATIE HARRIS

Most people say they want to make a bigger difference in life. We all have opportunities to do more, be happier, and find more meaning in our lives. But how might our stereotypes, expectations, and underlying assumptions keep us from achieving those desired outcomes?

Consider your definition of leadership. Have you ever fully articulated this definition for yourself? If you have, is it written down? If it is, are you acting on that definition in order to change your behavior and improve your outcomes?

No one has the ultimate definition of leadership, one that is somehow objectively correct, that everyone will agree on, and about which scholars will say, "This is it!" So, start with what *you* think leadership is, then inform your understanding with what others—such as practitioners and academics—think about leadership. Those practitioners and academics have done research, and they've read more than most others have about leadership. But you need to have your own definition of leadership as it will form the basis for your own actions.

Let's get started defining leadership by bringing to mind an early leadership experience (Activity 1.1). In one or two paragraphs, write the story of one of the first events or situations in which you exhibited leadership behavior. Then, reflect on why you chose the example you did. How does the story exemplify your personal take on leadership?

ACTIVITY 1.1 Your Earliest Leadership Story

When I ask people to do this, many have a hard time. They often don't know what they think about leadership, and I get answers like, "Well, I've never been in a leadership position," or, "I'm only a manager; I've never had the opportunity to lead." But whatever came to mind when you tried to recall your earliest leadership experience is actually quite revealing. It says a lot about what you think leadership is.

Self-awareness is one thing. Self-understanding is another. Self-understanding comes from analyzing the data of our experience so that we can understand the causes and consequences of our behaviors. To that end, think about why you chose the example you did and what it might reveal about the enduring values that you hold. It's very difficult to step up and make a choice to lead, so what is the enduring value that's driving your leadership behavior?

Volunteer Student Council

I was the president of my ninth-grade class. On a page in my yearbook from Gorman Junior High School in Colorado Springs, the heading states, "Student Council Has a Very Good Year." In addition to the photo of student council members, there's a group photo showing members of the "Volunteer Council." Did your junior high have a volunteer council? I'll bet that it didn't because as far as I know, I created it. Many of my fellow students wanted to contribute to making the school a better place, but they weren't members of student council. Maybe they hadn't been elected or even run for office, but they had a lot to offer, and there was no vehicle for participating in the existing system.

My first act of leadership was to create this volunteer student council, which allowed my fellow students to participate through volunteering on various committees tasked with building community, organizing events, inviting guest speakers, and representing diverse views. Why did I choose that particular example as my earliest leadership experience? And what does this experience reveal that's fundamental to my choosing leadership? Those are questions for you to ask yourself too.

In doing this exercise for myself, I discovered that when I step up to lead, I usually do so to level the playing field. And since ninth grade, when I've made a choice to lead, it has often been because I've wanted to provide opportunities that people otherwise wouldn't have had. Volunteer student council allowed people to contribute who wouldn't otherwise have had a seat at the table. It legitimized their opportunity to contribute.

Writing about your earliest leadership experience is a challenging task. However, in doing this, you have taken the first step toward greater self-understanding: you have collected data. The experience you record is descriptive data, and it is important because it is the raw data of your experience. And while it starts as a story, you can begin to analyze the underlying causes and consequences of your choice to lead. It will likely take several attempts before you are able to identify, analyze, and articulate the enduring value that served as a catalyst for your choice to lead. However, with dedicated effort, this exercise will help you to better understand what makes you step up and take the risk to create a better future.

Here is the earliest leadership experience offered by a college student named Alexandros:

> Senior year of high school, I had just lost the election for school president. I had high hopes and big dreams for what I wanted to do to make the school better, and I was not going to let that election prevent me from doing what I knew was good. For years, our pep rallies had been cancelled, but I wanted to enact positive change in the school, and my biggest idea was to bring the event back. I was not officially part of student government, but I still went to their meetings, and I spoke with administration almost every day. I came up with ideas and participated, and made the plans. I reached out to the community and garnered their support through a petition to bring the pep rally back. And when the principal finally declared that the pep rally would be scheduled, student council received the credit. While I would have liked to have been appreciated then and there for all of the effort I put in, I didn't mind that I had not because, in the end, I had

succeeded. I was still a leader because though I was behind the scenes, I still created change for the better. A true leader is a person who tries to bring people up, push the line in the right direction. And he doesn't necessarily have to be seen, or at the front of the line, but the one doing the push is really who everyone follows.

This story has some similarities to mine, but Alexandros distills his differently. In his story, despite losing the election, he still held to a vision for a better future at his school. He realized that he could pursue his goals without having the official title of class president. By engaging in leadership behavior, he succeeded in making the change that he had envisioned. And while the student council got the credit for bringing back pep rallies, he is the one who actually chose to lead and brought about that change.

These first two stories are about leading with and without a formal title. These next two stories have to do with courage.

For group learning, use Leadership Module 1.A: Early Leadership Story (45 Minutes)

Courage Is a Skill

Many people think of courage as an innate trait, believing that people are born with some predetermined amount of courage. I don't subscribe to overly personality-based explanations, so I don't consider courage to be an innate trait. There's a theory in social psychology called *cognitive dissonance,* which says that under certain conditions, you can start by changing your behavior and then your attitude will follow. By doing things that you consider courageous, you come to define yourself more as a more courageous person.

Skills benefit from practice, and changing your behavior is a skill. A good example of this can be seen in philanthropy. Foundations like to get a young person to make even small charitable donations early in life. That way, philanthropy becomes a regular practice and eventually one that is fundamental to that person's identity.

Your identity is linked to your outcomes, so the more you behave courageously and have courageous actions and outcomes, the more your attitude about yourself will change. Thus, you become more courageous. Even small steps taken in the direction of courage will serve you well.

Here's Connie's story:

My husband and I had taken our two young (early grade school) children to a combination hotel/indoor water park for a short winter weekend getaway. One night, early in the morning (maybe 2:00 a.m. or so), we were woken up by the sound of the hotel fire alarm going off. Trying not to panic, we grabbed coats and kids (left all the luggage—we were in our pajamas) and carried them down the stairs (no using elevators in a fire) to the ground floor where we headed for the nearest door out to the parking lot. There was a large crowd of people all standing bunched up in the hallway in front of the doorway, all wearing their pajamas and winter coats. With the alarm still blaring, I couldn't imagine why on earth people weren't getting out of the building, so with my daughter in my arms, I pushed my way up to the door vestibule area to find a young hotel employee with his arms outstretched and blocking the exit, loudly telling everyone to stay calm and that it was just a false alarm and that there was no reason to leave the building. My husband had come up behind me with our son. I just remember telling this young man that these were my children and it was my choice to leave and that we were not taking any chances. I pushed past him and we went out to our car. It was like a cork coming out of a bottle—as we were going to our car, I looked behind us and people were streaming out of the door behind me. I guess they just needed someone to take that step of thinking for themselves. It turned out in the end that it was indeed a false alarm, but we sat in the car with two overtired and upset kids in the cold and light snow with the engine running while firefighters checked the entire building. Eventually, the emergency response vehicles began leaving, and the hotel staff went car-to-car telling people it was okay to return. Afterward, I remember thinking to myself, *Holy cow, since when did you get so feisty?* for the way I pushed past that young employee's outstretched arms, but it felt right and good to do so. The memory of that event has really stuck with me. Motherhood makes you pretty tough and bold when it comes to protecting your kids. I didn't intend to "lead" anyone that night, but I did learn that exhibiting determination and conviction can inspire other people to make independent choices for themselves, even in the face of someone telling you "no."

Connie is an executive at a large firm—but she chose as her first leadership experience a story in which her main role was as a parent. She felt responsible for the safety of her children, and she went up against authority in order to behave in line with her responsibility. Her own choice, in the face of an emergency, surprised her. This reveals the importance of her sense of responsibility. The way she ends this story is also interesting: She looked behind her and saw that people were following her lead.

Which of your values surface in choosing leadership? For Connie, her values are responsibility, the courage to go against authority, and the consensual validation that followed. Her actions are in line with an interesting model of "followership" developed by Ira Chaleff, who argues that the courage to assume responsibility and to take moral action defines a courageous follower (see more on the importance of followership in Chapter 2).

Courage is a skill and skills benefit from practice.

Consider another story of courage as told by Sel, a longtime Booth colleague (in memory).

I enlisted in the army toward the end of WWII and was stationed at Fort Dix, New Jersey. There was a military band there, and I transferred into the band. There were no piano players, but I located one from another outfit, an all-black one. The army was segregated in those days. One of the first jobs I got for the band was [to play at] a dance to be held at the Officers' Club. At the entrance, since we weren't officers, we were asked for identification and reason for gaining entry.

I told him we were the band members there to play for the dance. He told us all to go in, except for the black guy. They [black people] weren't allowed. I tried a little cajoling, but it didn't work. At that point I made the decision that it was all or none of us and told him that there wouldn't be any music for the dance tonight. He notified someone inside the club, and an officer emerged. I reiterated my decision and waited. Finally, he said okay, we could all go in and provide the music. My guess is that our band was the first integrated unit in the military, and probably the first time a black man was allowed into the Officers' Club.

Sel's story demonstrated active resistance to racism. It took courage for an enlisted man to stand up to an officer. Sel's choice to keep his band together demonstrated his deeply held value of equality. It was based on the fact that the band was a cohesive unit that played together and stayed together regardless of any musician's race or skin color. And with his choice, Sel desegregated the Officers' Club, at least on that evening.

> $C = f(p^n)$. Where C is courage and p^n is exponential amounts of practice. —BARBARA PASSY

Changing the Conversation About Leadership

When we think of a "leader," what often comes to mind is a person who is bold, self-assured, and charismatic, or who has some of the other characteristics commonly associated with successful, high-profile leaders. Our sense of those characteristics stems from the work of the late personality psychologist Raymond B. Cattell, who in 1954 developed a model "to determine the traits which characterize an effective leader." Traits listed in Cattell's original article on this topic include emotional stability, dominance, enthusiasm, conscientiousness, social boldness, self-assurance, compulsiveness, intuitiveness, empathy, and charisma.

This summation of leadership has proven enduring. People remain firmly committed to the idea that there exists a leader personality type that has qualities such as those laid out by Cattell. To select and develop employees, businesses routinely measure "innate" dispositions using personality tests. The billion-dollar pre-hire testing industry sells a broad range of assessments—of questionable validity and reliability—to determine whether a candidate has these innate traits. Training programs often advise aspiring leaders to work on developing those areas of their personalities that don't measure up to the effective-leader personality type.

> **If you want to change your identity, change your behavior.**

While self-understanding and personal development are of obvious importance, there is a big problem with this approach. No one has ever figured out how people might go about acquiring an innate trait or whether attempts to develop such traits actually lead to more successful outcomes for individuals or their organizations. My goal is to refocus the discussion from innate traits to behaviors—from the noun "leader" to the verb "to lead"; from "manager" to "to manage"—in order to avoid leadership as a label and embrace it as a behavior.

The Leader Stereotype

When I teach, I ask my students for a list of words they associate with leaders. Inevitably and predictably, they produce a list of traits similar to those traits listed by Cattell and other personality-based theorists. My students' lists collectively tell the story of a mythic person, a change agent who has a vision for the future, breaks the mold, innovates passionately, and is volatile, courageous, and intoxicating.

Manager, of course, is the companion stereotype to leader. When I ask students to describe managers, they describe a relatively boring person who meets targets and stays busy with tasks at hand. This manager has no grand ideas or visions and will not disrupt the status quo.

These stereotypical views incorrectly imply that leaders and managers are born, not made. In reality, there is nothing innate or fixed about the qualities that make someone good at leading. The behaviors involved can be learned, honed, and encouraged through practice. When we use the word "leader" as a label, we do others and ourselves a disservice. There is substantial evidence that categorizing people creates biases in how they are perceived and distorts how others evaluate their performance.

Say you decide a woman in your department is an excellent manager because she is capable, good with colleagues, and very reliable. She likes consensus and is a team builder. But she is not an extrovert and doesn't seem to exhibit those personality traits you associate with leaders. By labeling her a manager, you might miss that she also has the capacity for leadership behaviors—and you may limit her opportunity to demonstrate leadership.

Similarly, you may consider yourself a leader because you have big ambitions and grand ideas. You may be unhappy with the status quo and determined to do something about it. Once you label yourself a leader, you may discount the importance of making this quarter's numbers or neglect important relationships. If you do, you may soon find you lack the capacity, record, or relationships you need to engage in effective leadership behaviors.

> **A journey of a thousand miles begins with a single step.** —LAOZI

For group learning, use Leadership Module 1.B: Leadership Myth-Busting (30 Minutes)

When Were You a Champion?

To understand the gist of this book, it's essential to understand what I mean by being a champion. I don't use this word in the sense of being the "winner," as of some contest, but rather as an advocate for something important to you. You are a champion whenever you are leading and managing to achieve your goals. Here is what my former student Shilpa told me about her earliest leadership experience, which shows what a champion she already was at sixteen years of age.

My earliest leadership memory is tutoring Ashley. Ashley was a first-grader in my neighborhood who needed a personal tutor to help her complete her work for school. She was a bright girl, with so much zeal and fire in her, and my job was to channel that energy into her homework and projects so she could move to the second grade. My sixteen-year-old self thought this would be a cakewalk. I love to teach! I love school! Kids love me! No brainer, right? I had never been more wrong. For the first few months, I approached tutoring Ashley after school like, well, a tutor. Every day after school, I went over to her home; I sat with her at her kitchen table and asked her what she learned in school that day. Every day, I got an annoyed glare and a mumbled, "Nothing." I would beg her, plead with her to pay attention, celebrate with high-fives when she actually applied herself in hopes that she would find this fun. And every day it was a battle. Her attention span was extremely short, and it seemed she found pleasure in intentionally getting the answers incorrect and watching me get frustrated. Worst of all, Ashley certainly wasn't retaining the information—she had no stake in the game. After three months of tutoring, Ashley had her mid-year report card, and she was failing.

I knew the issue wasn't intelligence. Academics were boring to Ashley. She wanted to play with her friends after school, not sit down at her kitchen table for hours and do math and reading exercises. I realized I needed to do two things: Get her to know me as Shilpa and make studying fun. Ashley loved sports—especially basketball. So, we moved from the kitchen table to the basement, where she had her hoop set up. Then, I made up rules for my newly formed tutoring method. For every page read correctly, Ashley got to take a free-throw shot. For every two pages read correctly without stopping, Ashley got to play me with some semblance of a full-court press and a chance to shoot a three-pointer. Finally, in between reading pages and taking free throws, we got to know each other as people. She started to let me in on who her friends were at school, and I told her about my friends as well. We talked about what she wanted to be when she grew up (a WNBA player of course), and I tried to get her to see how succeeding in school would help her with that goal. I learned more and more about Ashley, her motivations, her fears—and most of all—what an incredibly intelligent and sharp little girl she was. She amazed me with her ability to negotiate for an extra free-throw shot if she combined her reading exercises with math ones and her inherent sense of always knowing what she wanted—never wavering for a moment. I knew then there wasn't anything that she couldn't do—I just needed her to see that.

Ashley ended the year with a B average report card. I'd like to think that Ashley learned a lot from me that year, but I actually learned the most from her. I also learned a lot about leadership. That year made me realize that you can have the clearest of visions, the best of intentions, and even have authority, but that doesn't mean people are going to listen to you. Leadership is as much about building relationships with others and recognizing their qualities and strengths as much as it is about being agile in the face of continuous challenges to, eventually, show people how to fly on their own.

Just like Shilpa, every champion needs to know when to manage and when to lead. It was not enough for Shilpa to have the vision for Ashley. She had to find the way to achieve it

Every idea, no matter how obvious, needs a champion.

by practicing management, implementing her plans in a creative way, adapting, and persisting until she achieved her goal. Like any champion, she combined leading and managing. I use the term *champion* throughout this book because it is the perfect way to understand and practice what this book is all about.

> There are loud leaders and quiet ones, strong, take-charge leaders and gently persuasive ones . . . What sort of leader do you want to be?
> —HAROLD LEAVITT

For group learning, use Leadership Module 1.B: Labels (30 Minutes)

Leadership Should Be More Verb than Noun

Labeling yourself and others as a champion can help move you past the limitations of our stereotypes. This term is inclusive because it does not apply only to people at the top of an organization. In fact, a person does not need to manage others in order to be considered a champion. Substituting this term for "leader" might help us better understand that everyone in an organization can be a champion. We all have the choice to engage in both types of behavior—managing and leading.

You will have more success if you have a more complex understanding of management and leadership as behaviors, not personality traits. Recognize that what matters is not whether you match up to some template of a leader personality; what matters is how you choose to behave. Unlike traits, it's our behaviors that form the basis for skills, and skills benefit from practice. A leadership-type behavior is forward looking; it is concerned with a vision to change the present and create a better future. A management-type behavior is focused on the present, concerned with stability in the here and now. Champions practice both behaviors, so choosing which behavior to practice at any given point in time becomes a central challenge. But you can make this choice by developing your courage, wisdom, and capacity.

Kurt Lewin, the founding father of social psychology, offered a version of the following equation in his 1936 book, *Principles of Topological Psychology:* $B = f(PS)$. This states that behavior (B) is a function (f) of the person (P) and their environment or situation (S). I introduce this equation in my classes to help students understand the usefulness of situation-based explanations of behavior as opposed to personality-based explanations.

For over thirty years, I have taught my students how to think more like a social psychologist. My advice is, if you want to change someone's behavior, try to change that person's situation, not the person. Champions have less control over others' personality attributes than they do over external factors such as rewards, peers, and physical space.

> **Leadership is one of the most observed and least understood phenomena on Earth.**
>
> —JAMES MACGREGOR BURNS

The challenge is to keep Lewin's equation in mind. Your choice to lead or manage should be based on both (P) and (S), where (P) does not represent personality alone but includes your values and goals. Some situations, (S), may call for having grand visions for creating new realities. Those situations may require behavior often associated with leadership, such as making difficult choices, taking risks, and tuning out naysayers. Other situations, however, may call for behaviors that maintain the status quo or execute a long-term plan. These behaviors can earn you trust from the people whose support you may need when you decide to make a different choice at a more critical juncture.

For group learning, use Leadership Module 1.C: Think Like a Social Psychologist (30 Minutes)

ACTIVITY 1.2 Zero-Draft Leadership Definition

_____

_____

_____

_____

For group learning, use Leadership Module 1.D: Zero-Draft Leadership Definition (20 Minutes)

CHAPTER 2
Defining Leading and Managing

For group learning, use Leadership Module 2.A: Juxtapositions (20 Minutes)

List some words you associate with leadership and juxtapose equivalent words that you associate with management. Given that champions engage in both management and leadership, do your best to select words that are roughly similar in terms of how positive they are, as in these examples. Continue to fill in the columns below before moving to the next page.

ACTIVITY 2.1 Juxtaposing Leadership and Management

LEADERSHIP	MANAGEMENT
Change	Stability
Future	Present
There	Here

Over the years, I have done this exercise many times in my Leadership Capital class. Table 2.1 that follows contains a selection of what my executive MBA students have listed in each column. What pairs do you find interesting, intriguing, and worthy of further reflection?

> **Leaders optimize upside opportunity; managers minimize downside risk.** —BOB SUTTON

Table 2.1: **Leadership and Management**

LEADERSHIP	MANAGEMENT
Change/Movement	Stability/Status Quo
Value Transfer	Value Alignment
Intrinsic Motivation	Extrinsic Motivation
Expert & Referent Power	Legitimate Power
Composer	Conductor
Art	Science
Inspiration	Instruction
Heart	Head
Subjective	Objective
Builds Momentum	Mobilizes Energy
Development of Capacity	Use of Capacity
Rule-breaking	Rule-following
Long-term	Short-term
Telescope	Binoculars
Follower	Direct Reports
Passion	Stamina
Innovation	Problem-solving
Start	Finish
Mindful	Soulful
Volatile/Unpredictable	Constant/Predictable
Chaos/Stormy Seas	Order/Calm Seas
Where should we go?	How should we get there?
The Promised Land	The Carrot and Stick
Quieter	Louder
Tomorrow	Today
Creates Ambiguity	Reduces Ambiguity
Vision-centric	People-centric
Courageous	Encouraging
Asks Why	Asks How
Policy-breaking	Policy-setting
Purpose	Reason
Defining Success	Measuring Success
Fights Wars	Fights Battles
Intoxicating	Sober
Green Pen	Red Pen
Suspenders	Belt
Lion	Tiger

Let's discuss a few of these examples. Some people have thought about leadership as art and management as science. Which is more important, art or science? In my opinion, they're equally important. Some people have thought about leadership as tomorrow and management as today. Of course, both of those are important, just as management and leadership are each important.

Passion versus stamina is another interesting pairing. Champions need stamina to manage. When managing, you're in the present, fighting fires and getting things done. But champions also need passion to fuel their belief in a better tomorrow and to communicate their vision to others. Who is to say which is more important, stamina or passion?

Someone once told me, "I want to be a leader; if only I had a vision." The image that came to my mind when hearing that was of someone in a constant hallucinatory state. When I talk to young people, sometimes they'll ask me, "I want to be a leader—where do I get a vision?" as though we could go to the store and buy a ready-made vision off the shelf.

> " I have called executives those knowledge workers, managers or individual professionals, who are expected by virtue of their position or their knowledge to make decisions in the normal course of their work that have significant impact on the performance and results of the whole. —PETER DRUCKER

We can't go around seeing visions everyday—we also need to get things done! As the late management professor Douglas McGregor said, "Management is about getting things done through people." We need both stamina and passion, just as we need both today and tomorrow.

The intoxicating versus sober pairing is similar to that of passion versus stamina. What does it mean to be intoxicated all the time? You can't spend every day leading people into an unknown future—you'd wear everyone out, including yourself. Choosing leadership is about deciding when to take the risk to change the future because once you enter the unknown, you'd better be sober enough to make your vision of the future a present reality.

Another juxtaposition that I like is leadership is a lion while management is a tiger. Imagine being a tiger. You're in the jungle surrounded by trees, right there in the thick of it. But now imagine being a lion, in the plains where you have a line of sight all the way out to the horizon.

We could ask which is better, the lion (as leadership) or the tiger (as management)? But these animals live in completely different habitats. They would never meet, and we don't know who would win in a competition between them. Just as is the case with management and leadership, neither animal is better than the other. They're different. Both tigers and lions are noble, important animals. Hopefully thinking about how you could juxtapose leading and managing helps you better articulate your definition of leadership.

You can also talk with your children using such juxtapositions with my children's picture book, called *Leadership Is...* It can help you engage young children in a conversation around what it means to lead.

Let children tell you why the moon is leading and the sun is managing. You will be surprised by how interesting and creative they are. Or just let them talk about the moon and the sun, and an insight about leading and managing might arrive later. Mainly, just have fun, let them lead the way, and simply manage the situation.

The little book is a family-and-friends project with volunteer translators around the world helping to make *Leadership Is...* available in the languages of my students. Readers can download it as a free PDF and choose from among more than thirty languages—and counting *(choosingleadershipbook.com/little-champions)*. Together, we can change the conversation around leadership for young children.

> **The secret to happiness is to see all the marvels of the world and never to forget the drops of oil in the spoon.** —PAULO COELHO

Managing Is Noble

When you are managing, you need people's heads. It's great but unnecessary to also have their hearts. You need people to understand what you are trying to accomplish, whether it's making the production schedule or getting something else done. They don't need to believe deeply in the task at hand, but they need to have the information and tools to get the job done.

When managing, you are using *legitimate power*. You have a title, and people will often do what you ask of them because you are the boss. As the boss, you also have "reward power," the ability to provide positive outcomes and take away negative ones, and "coercive power," the ability to provide negative outcomes. When I'm the boss, I can reward you with a nice assignment, a bonus, or more access. I can also take away a high-visibility assignment.

People often think that management is less important than leadership. Do your best not to buy into that stereotype. Management provides the platform for future growth. If we don't have good management, we can't have a future. When managing, we are helping people feed their families, educate their children, and live their dreams. Managing is noble.

> " Pathfinding is about the future we want to create rather than the one we try to discover . . . [it] is very much about you, about who you are, what you value and what you believe is worth doing. —HAROLD LEAVITT

Capital L or Lowercase l

Most of the time, you are maintaining or enhancing the status quo, and that's just fine. In fact, that's the right thing to be doing. But every once in a while, as a champion, you make a risky choice to be a trailblazer. And your vision for a better tomorrow usually comes from the fact that you are somehow dissatisfied with today's status quo. When you've made the choice to lead, you are still the same champion who was managing, is now leading, and will soon manage again.

There are two ways to think about choosing leadership: with a capital *L* or with a lowercase *l*. Capital L represents a big, transformational change, such as starting a new venture. Activity 2.2 asks you to think about capital *L* leadership, while lowercase *l* represents the smaller choices you make every day to create a better future. The distinction between *L* and *l* is often lost in many seminars, books, articles, and discussions about leadership.

ACTIVITY 2.2 Capital L Leadership Story

What's your story of leadership with a capital *L*?

Here's my capital *L* leadership story: I had been teaching at the University of Chicago for a couple of years when the dean at Northwestern's Kellogg School of Management asked me to return to teach MBAs and design executive education certificate programs. Aside from designing social psychology experiments, there is nothing that I find more creative than designing educational programs. This was 1995, and there was no opportunity for me to do this at Booth because at the time we did not offer executive education. So I met with my dean, Robin Hogarth, to give my resignation. When I explained why I was leaving, Robin asked, "Why not do the same job here? Make me a proposal."

Booth hadn't been interested in short, certificate programs until that point because the school was focused on longer, degree-granting programs. But I took Robin's challenge to heart and thought it would be great to create my own "start-up" rather than help to run an already well-oiled machine. I visited five senior faculty members who I worried might be opposed to my starting a non-degree venture and asked for them not to resist my efforts. I promised them I would create executive education that would be uniquely Booth—small, serious, and solid.

I declined Kellogg's offer and explained to Dean Don Jacobs there that I had the opportunity to stay at Booth and create a start-up focused on customized executive education. Robin opened the door for me, and I stepped through it. I happened to be the one who took the risk and chose leadership. That's how I started the business of custom executive education at the Booth School of Business.

The distinction between *L* and *l* highlights the myth that everything in leadership has to do with a capital *L*. Choosing leadership can also involve small choices, the kind we make every day. When we lead with a more expansive definition of leadership, we will engage in more leadership behaviors and allow those around us to engage in more types of activities that create a better future.

When Leadership Comes In

> Winter 1990. About ten boys standing behind the pavilion eager to start the cross-country season, but there is no teacher. The sport didn't get much attention in our school. After a few jokes and some horseplay, I realized the other would-be athletes were looking at me. Why me? I'm not oldest, I'm definitely not an academic senior. But, I love running. It puts a smile on my face. I love motivating people to challenge and improve themselves.
>
> Couple of deep breaths; in through the nose, out through the mouth, as described in the *Runner's World* magazine. Come on guys, I shouted! Let's go out to the Dragon's Back (as the notorious hill was known) and do some hill repeats. Don't worry, we go out at an easy pace and we will stick in a group. Follow me!

As my former student Jake's leadership story demonstrates, he had to have confidence in his vision, and he swayed both the heads *and hearts* of his fellow students on that winter day. Those boys needed to believe in his vision of the future. Pursuing that vision is risky for you and for anyone who is following you. This is because they need to follow you to an unknown place without being afraid of falling off a cliff—or in this case, tumbling down the notorious Dragon's Back.

When managing, you need the heads of your followers because they have to understand what you're trying to accomplish. But when you make a choice to lead, to change the future, your confidence and beliefs come into play. You haven't been to the future yet, so you don't actually know that your vision of that future exists.

 There's a time for daring and there's a time for caution, and a wise man understands which is called for.
—JOHN KEATING (ROBIN WILLIAMS), FROM THE MOVIE *DEAD POETS SOCIETY*

There are two types of power that are unrelated to title or position, and these are the power types you rely on when choosing leadership. *Referent power* is when people "refer" to you. This is your ability to be a role model. There are as many types of referent power as there are people, and whatever it is that makes people want to follow you, that's your source of referent power. When people look up to you, they believe in you and want to help you succeed. It is the closest thing we have to that mythical notion of charisma. *Expert power* is the ability to move people in your direction because of your expertise, knowledge, and experience. When you bring referent and expert power together, people look up to you, want to be like you, and believe in you.

When people talk about leadership, they often use the word "charisma." But the suggestion that you need charisma to lead is a myth that can bring a lot of grief. Whoever is your charismatic ideal—whether it's Martin Luther King, Mother Teresa, or anyone else—you will never be able to match up to that ideal. And if you think you need that person's level of charisma in order to be a leader, you're bound to fall short and be disappointed.

When you hear people use the word charisma, think about it as referent power. And remember that there are as many different kinds of referent power as there are people doing this book. Your task is to figure out what it is about you that makes people want to follow you. If you need to imitate or to try acting like somebody else for a while, that's okay. You can fake it 'til you make it, as they say. But at some point, you'll have to figure out how to be yourself. Don't fake it too long.

> **Example is the best lesson there is.** —ELEANOR ROOSEVELT

Using Both the Map and the Compass

When you are managing, you're in the here and now. You are making the budget, meeting the street's expectations, and getting things done. The terrain is charted, and you manage as though following a map. By contrast, when you choose to lead, there's no map. The most you can have is a sense of direction, such as that provided by a compass, and use it to chart a path to an unknown place.

The University of Michigan's Karl Weick has said that managers use maps and leaders use compasses. I see it differently: the same champion must keep both a compass and a map handy.

Go back to the terms you wrote for the activity at the beginning of this chapter. Did your words convey that management is low level and leadership is high level? This is a great exercise to help you think about your initial default and how to unfreeze that default, change it, and recognize leadership and management as being more equivalent. Think of yourself as a champion who often manages and sometimes leads, you'll start seeing past the stereotypes of leadership as heroic and management as mundane. It's an exercise that can help you "refreeze" your notions around leading and managing in a different place. This is hard, but it will get easier with practice. Remember, skills benefit from practice.

For group learning, use Leadership Module 2.B: The Map and Compass (30 Minutes)

Three Stages of Change

I should explain what I mean by refreezing. Let's return to Kurt Lewin, the founding father of a social psychology. Lewin proposed a three-step model to explain change that involves unfreezing, changing, and refreezing. In order to change, you need to:

1. **UNFREEZE:** Understand the need and find the motivation to change.
2. **CHANGE:** Move toward a different behavior.
3. **REFREEZE:** Solidify the change and establish that new behavior as the norm.

What I'm trying to do with these initial leadership stories is to defrost some of your frozen ideas about what it means to lead. At some point, you're defrosted, but you will still be semisolid. And where will you refreeze? My hope is that the "future you" will freeze in a better place. Will you be a new and improved self, or will you revert back to the old you because that self is familiar? It's up to you.

I have two stories about Lewin's three stages of change and about refreezing in particular. One story doubles as marital advice. You change every day as a result of who you talk to, what you do, and what you experience. If you don't bring your partner along with you on this daily journey, at some point they'll look at you, see a stranger, and wonder what happened to the person they used to know and love. A friend once told me that sometimes the reason people get divorced is not that they want a new partner but that they themselves want to be a different person, and their partner doesn't allow them to change. Many years ago, I promised to do everything possible to ensure that my husband and I brought each other along every day as we changed. We have been happily married for over three decades.

The other story is about prison, namely recidivism in the prison population. In addition to punishment, incarceration is also meant to provide rehabilitation. Society takes offenders and puts them into a radically different environment; by doing this, we're unfreezing the offenders. At some point, we release them back into society, but they are still semisolid at that point. We put them back in their old environment, and unsurprisingly many refreeze back where they were, not as the new and improved versions of themselves.

The moment of change is really just a point in time. Where will you refreeze? When you finish this book, will you refreeze as the person you were, or will you refreeze as a new and improved version of yourself? How will you create a strong environment around the new you to help refreeze in a better place?

Think like a social psychologist: Behavior is a function of a person and a situation. In understanding behavior, don't underestimate the power of situations. What are the factors in your environment affecting your behavior? Create a strong situation around you to sustain your change.

It helps to create a strong environment with a critical mass of people who understand and support the new you.

Effective Followers

For group learning, use Leadership Module 2.C: The First Follower (15 Minutes)

Throughout much of this book, I present the argument that there are two key champion behaviors, leading and managing, and at any point in time you have to decide which to practice. But there is a third important behavior: *following*. And effective following is vital.

We don't often hear about followership, likely because of stereotypical notions or ideas about what it means to follow—that is, a behavior much less important than managing and leading. Despite the thousands of articles about leadership, only a handful exist about followership. Abraham Zaleznik focuses on followership with regard to the traits of dominance (versus submissiveness) and activity (versus passivity). Barbara Kellerman's followership model focuses on level of engagement. Ira Chaleff's focuses on the courage to challenge.

In the same vein, just as we tend to think of leaders as having traits suited to that activity, so do we tend to think of followers as being inherently suited for following. Worse, we tend to think of followers as people who are passive and uncritical—"sheep," as Carnegie Mellon's Robert Kelley calls them. But passive, uncritical followers are ineffective, whereas effective followers are engaged and thinking critically about the tasks at hand. In fact, active engagement and critical thinking are two dimensions of followership identified by Kelley's 1988 article "In Praise of Followers," from the *Harvard Business Review*. Figure 2.1 illustrates this concept.

How do you know when to follow and when to lead? You lead when following isn't fun anymore. —RANDY LEWIS

Figure 2.1: **Effective Followers**

A thin line separates leading and following. The person considered the smartest one in the room is not necessarily leading. In the same vein, whoever is considered "the person with the answers" or "the traffic cop" is not necessarily leading. Consider Lena's story:

> One summer while I was on a break from high school, my family went on vacation to Turkey. My mom and I went on a sightseeing boat trip one evening along with a few other tourists. A while later, the engine of this rustic boat broke down. The only employee on board, the boat's captain, was at a loss of what to do, and back then cell phones didn't exist. As the captain tried to tinker around with the boat's engine, I became convinced that we needed to act fast as it was getting dark, and we were drifting into the open ocean.

As the other passengers became more anxious, I took charge and spoke to the captain on behalf of the group. I saw a large yacht at a distance and convinced the captain to swim up and seek help from that yacht. My main objective was to ensure that everyone was safe and then to worry about fixing the boat. As a result, we were brought on board the yacht, and then safely transported back to shore.

This story illustrates that champions must speak up for what they believe is the right thing to do, persevere, and take risks as well as responsibility for others' wellbeing. Additionally, leadership is called upon when stakes are high, and champions appreciate the value of their challenging experiences over time.

Activity 2.3 asks you to reflect on the importance of being a good follower.

> **When faith is present in the leader, it communicates itself to followers with powerful effect. In the conventional mode people want to know whether the followers believe in the leader; a more searching question is whether the leader believes in the followers.** —JOHN GARDNER

ACTIVITY 2.3 What Makes You an Effective Follower?

Under what conditions are you engaged and thinking critically?

_____

_____

_____

_____

ACTIVITY 2.3 What Makes You an Effective Follower? (Continued)

How can you increase critical thinking in the people you work with and who work for you?

_____

_____

_____

_____

How can you increase active engagement in the people you work with and who work for you?

_____

_____

_____

_____

What does it mean to contribute?

_____

_____

_____

_____

 Are you a leader or a follower? Try asking this question of a dozen people and record their answers. Then analyze their perspectives and think about the implications of using these labels. What you learn may surprise you.

Back to "Champion"

To help defrost the labels of manager and leader, substitute my umbrella term champion. Other people have handled this labeling problem in different ways. My mentor at Stanford University, the late, great Harold Leavitt, introduced the compound word *manager–leader*. He used it in his writing in order to communicate that you are the same person who happens to be either leading or managing at any given moment. I've had other people tell me, "I just use the word *leader*, and everyone knows that I mean manager and leader," or vice versa. The problem is that people talk about leaders *and* managers as if they are different people—or worse, different species—instead of the same people who are doing different things at different times.

And just as labels can affect your thinking and actions, so can your definition of leadership. If your definition reflects the commonly held stereotypes, it might be constraining your own choices. It might also be limiting the choices of the people around you, compounding the bias, all because you have a too-narrow definition of what it means to lead.

At the end of the first chapter, you wrote your zero-draft definition of leadership. Now that we're at the end of Chapter 2, it's time for your first draft.

What do you think is the gist, the core essence, of leadership? Marvin Minsky, the father of artificial intelligence, once said that point of view is worth 80 IQ points. You can raise your IQ just by developing your own perspective. What's your own point of view?

ACTIVITY 2.4 First-Draft Leadership Definition

_____

_____

_____

_____

Codifying one's thinking is an important step in inventing oneself. The most difficult way to do it is by thinking about thinking—it helps to speak or write your thoughts. Writing is the most profound way of codifying your thoughts, the best way of learning who you are and what you believe.
—WARREN BENNIS

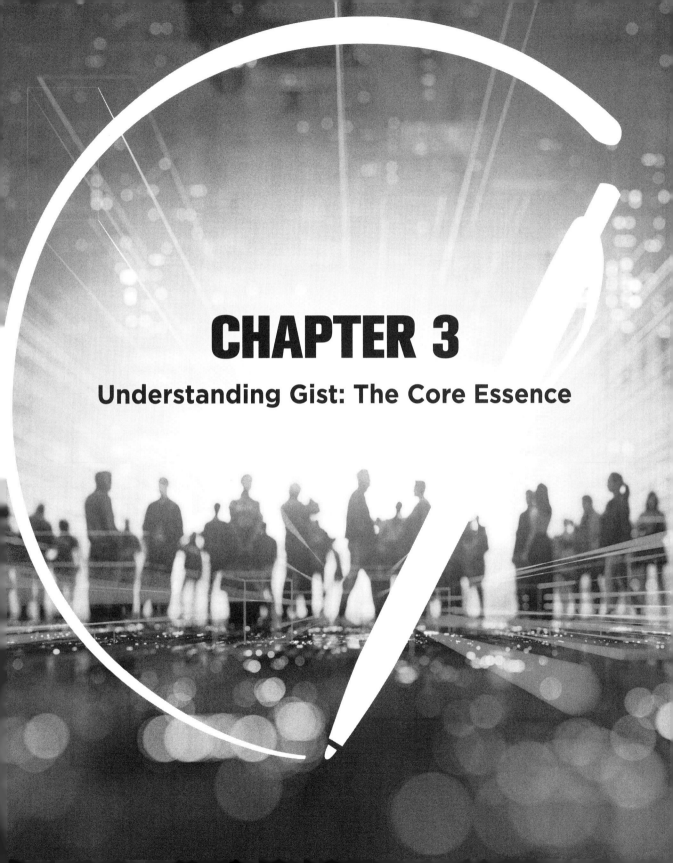

CHAPTER 3

Understanding Gist: The Core Essence

> Most people do not accumulate a body of experience. Most people go through life undergoing a series of happenings, which pass through their systems undigested. Happenings become experiences when they are digested, when they are related to general patterns and synthesized.
> —SAUL D. ALINSKY

One of the most important and difficult concepts you'll tackle in this book is *gist*. This is somewhat ironic because gist is, ultimately, simple almost by definition. Gist means "core essence" and refers, in the sense I use it, to something that's fundamental, deep, and meaningful to you.

You can find gist in just about anything. For example, what do you see as the core essence of leadership? What is the core essence of your identity? What is the core essence of a speech you just listened to, or of this chapter? Finding your own answers to these questions are key to your leadership development.

To understand gist, think of a play. When you're at the theater, what the characters on stage say to each other is descriptive—their words describe their situation. But what does the conversation tell us about the characters' relationship? What is it meant to reveal? Why did the playwright choose those particular words? To understand gist, we have to go beyond description and try to understand *why*. This requires us to engage in analysis.

A lot of people think that they need more knowledge in order to become wiser. But knowledge is like butter in the hot sun. You won't understand leadership by collecting books on a shelf; you have to extract your own unique understanding from those books, as well as from other materials and experiences. What's important is not how much you read but how much you understand in your own terms. This is the difference between knowledge and wisdom.

Theatergoers experiencing the same play can have different impressions of it. Some people might even take opposing views of the playwright's intentions. This is why it's important to customize your learning in leadership: your gist may not be the same as someone else's. You have to do your own analysis in order to understand what *you* consider the core essence. You have to find your own gist. This may sound simple, but it's not simplistic. This is why we're spending this chapter learning about this concept, and we'll spend the remaining chapters further exploring ways to get at gist.

This chapter began with a quote from Saul Alinsky discussing the importance of experiences. A lot of people say experience is the best teacher, but just because you have an experience doesn't mean you will learn anything from it. When I read Alinsky's quote for the first time, I realized why we don't learn automatically from an experience: we're often having happenings instead. Those happenings are much like the dialogue in a play: they are just words. You have to process those words to understand your gist. Otherwise you're just accumulating knowledge and information—like placing books on a shelf—but not becoming wiser.

Self-understanding is a key skill for choosing leadership—for deciding when to manage and when to lead. It allows you to be confident in your choices and aware of the impact you can have in motivating and inspiring other people. Central to the gist of your own experience are your values and goals, so the ultimate aim of this lesson is to help you find your own gist. Analyze and understand your core essence in order to articulate your values and goals and convey them to others.

This I Believe

For group learning, use Leadership Module 3.A: This I Believe (30 minutes)

Detailing your earliest leadership experience (Activity 1.1, page 13) prepared you for capturing gist. In that exercise, you had to think about your core essence when you explored why you made a certain choice. Now, think further in order to write about one of your cornerstone beliefs, one that you think is worthy of further articulation. This will likely be an enduring, core value that fueled your earliest leadership experience, and which has also been a driving force in many of your decisions and actions throughout your life.

Think about the gist revealed by Laura as she explored the thread between her earliest and most recent leadership experiences.

In the 1960s, the *Chicago Tribune* newspaper ran a series of phonics lessons for children in the Sunday comics section where the lessons used story, color imagery, humor, and even acting suggestions for adults who wished to make the ideas come to life for pre-kindergarteners. I remember with great affection my mother sitting on the "good" living room sofa while I sat at her feet to go through each letter's lesson. It was on the letter "L" lesson that I suggested my younger sister join our sessions, even though she was two years younger than I was. I argued that her name began with an "L" just as mine did and that she was so smart she would surely enjoy the gift of independence in early reading attempts. We doubled the fun of our "one room, one mom-teacher, and two student schoolhouse" that day and began a shared family love of reading.

Leadership to me still is being curious about others' viewpoints and contributions and letting them know you're confident they'll be an important part of the conversation.

Fast forward. Four decades later, I love using the Socratic method of thoughtful dialogue with a team. So when convening a group of individuals, authoring a charter of roles has long been my primary task. Recently, I was asked to chair a project team commissioned by the director to enhance our safety training. Other project teams were also launched (at the same meeting) that day to "fix" safety. All in there were about thirty senior leaders within six teams ready to assemble, write reports, and announce recommendations in about six weeks' time. From the first meeting, I asked my team if they were okay with asking the other five teams to work on various topics together, as there was significant overlap in both inputs and deliverables. I couldn't imagine all of us completing our work whilst strewn all about the campus not talking to each other.

If we were truly interested in using data and research to change behaviors and improve outcomes based on common understanding, then we would need to have large-group, small-group, and one-on-one conversations. To my way of thinking, we would have to have a combined point of view final presentation to the board in order to actually make a difference in the safety story.

Laura believes in bringing others into the conversation; what do you believe?

 Beliefs are choices. No one has authority over your personal beliefs. Your beliefs are in jeopardy only when you don't know what they are. —JAY ALLISON

ACTIVITY 3.1 This I Believe

This activity is inspired by National Public Radio's *This I Believe*, which describes itself as "an international organization engaging people in writing and sharing essays describing the core values that guide their daily lives." The organization was inspired by a popular 1950s radio show with that name.

The idea is to write an essay of 350–500 words that sums up your personal beliefs and explains their significance. This is intended to serve as a point of departure as you work to both develop and communicate personal knowledge. These writing guidelines are a slightly tweaked version of those posted on https://ThisIBelieve.org.

1. **TELL A STORY:** Be specific. Take your belief out of the ether and ground it in the events of your life. Consider moments when belief was formed or tested or changed. Think of your own experience, work, and family, and tell of the things you know that no one else does. Your story need not be heart-warming or gut-wrenching—it can even be funny—but it should be *real*. Make sure your story ties to the essence of your daily life philosophy and the shaping of your beliefs.

2. **BE BRIEF:** Your statement should be between 350 and 500 words. That's about three minutes when read aloud at your natural pace.

3. **NAME YOUR BELIEF:** Rather than writing a list of your core beliefs, consider focusing on one, because 500 words are used up quickly. You should be able to name or explain your belief in a sentence or two.

4. **BE POSITIVE:** Avoid preaching or editorializing. Tell us what you do, not what you don't believe. Avoid speaking in the editorial "we." Make your essay about you; speak in the first person.

5. **BE PERSONAL:** Write in words and phrases that are comfortable for you to speak. Read your essay aloud several times, and each time edit and simplify it until you find the words, tone, and story that truly echo your belief.

Use the space provided on the following page to begin drafting your essay.

ACTIVITY 3.1 This I Believe (continued)

With this exercise, you are accomplishing two things. First, it helps you recognize, articulate, and explore what's important to you. Because the essay is only 500 words at most, you have to work hard to make those words count. The editing process you'll need in order to fit this limit is crucial. When you have to boil something down to 500 words, you're practicing how to get to the gist.

Second, this essay is also an exercise in communicating gist. This is not a private, confidential essay that you have written for yourself. It's for you to share with other people, if you choose. It's a vehicle you can use to communicate your cornerstone values to others.

For group learning, use Leadership Module 3.B: Definition of Success (20 minutes)

Understanding and communicating are key leadership skills. When leading, you need to be able to recognize the gist of something and then be able to communicate that gist to your peers. Harvard's Eric McNulty recommends a similar exercise he calls "The Personal Manifesto." It is a less structured collection of beliefs and quotes designed to help you connect to your personal definition of success through an intense, ongoing conversation with yourself.

What is your personal definition of success?

_____

_____

_____

These activities ask you to begin exploring the gist of your self-knowledge. With continued practice, you should ultimately be able to process the gist of many important things. Getting at the core essence is a lifelong process.

Over the years, I have asked many students of leadership to write their personal credos, and it has been my privilege to read about their beliefs. Students have written essays about carrying their own luggage, wearing colorful socks, and listening to Phil Collins. There were some seemingly outrageous essay topics, yet they all conveyed profound lessons in self-understanding.

Consider one of my favorites, by Benjamin Johnson, an executive MBA student. Titled "The Chicago Cubs Will, One Day, Win the World Series," it was written prior to the Cubs actually winning the World Series in 2016, for the first time since 1908.

> I have a friend who likes to joke that there are two forms of acceptable child abuse in America: raising a world-class gymnast and raising a Cubs fan.
>
> To an outsider, there is good amount of truth to this joke. Who wants to be a Cubs fan? To be the lovable loser. To be cursed . . . by a goat. To be always waiting until next year.
>
> I've always looked at it differently. In a way that I imagine must be somewhat related to how a caribou calf can walk along with its herd within minutes of being born, a fan of the Chicago Cubs has (at least until very recently) some innate capabilities that normally take years to properly develop.
>
> The bestselling author John C. Maxwell wrote a book titled *Failing Forward*. Its premise is that most people are not prepared to deal with failure. It is 224 pages long. I've never read it. I don't need to read it. I'm prepared for failure. It is not that I like to lose. Even Cubs fans don't *like* to lose, but we know that it happens. It happens even when you've done everything you were supposed to do. It happens even when you are expected to win. It's not the end of the world. You take what you can learn from the loss and try again next year.
>
> Being a born loser teaches you another pretty important lesson: winning is not everything. Happiness is not defined by banners, by rings, by winnings. Happiness is a friendly home. It is a beautiful summer day in Chicago. It is surrounding yourself with good people. It is the love of the game.
>
> Losing for 108 years in a row teaches you the difference between a hope and a wish. A wish is something that comes into your mind after you realize that you've made a mistake.

> You wish you listened to your wife and packed that damn rain jacket.
>
> You hope for something big. You hope with patience. You hope with grit. You defer gratification because you believe that one day, when the Cubs do finally win the World Series, it will be worth it.

To me, this essay is about maintaining hope even when there's plenty of evidence that suggests you should abandon it. In this case, 108 years of experience suggested rooting for a different team.

That's my interpretation of the gist of this essay, and I think it's beautiful. I'm also a Cubs fan, so I have my biases.

? **QUESTION**
What is the gist of Benjamin's essay for you?

_____

_____

_____

_____

Choice as Possibility

Gist is about deciding what something means. That can be true quite literally. You have probably seen reversible figures, which are ambiguous drawings that represent different perspectives. For example, you may be familiar with the picture that can be seen as a duck or a rabbit, and perhaps you've seen the line drawing that looks like a young woman or an old woman. My favorite reversible figure is one that can be seen as either a vase or as two faces in profile:

Figure 3.1: **Reversible Figure**

Do you see the vase or two faces? We usually see darker images on a lighter background, like the black letters on this white page. But in the case of the vase, the figure is light on a dark background, so it reverses the typical figure-ground relationship.

You decide what you see.

The reversible figure demonstrates that perception is a choice, as are most of our behaviors. When we talk about leading and managing, we're often talking about complex and multifaceted behaviors. But this image reveals that we typically have more choices than we recognize. You may see one option in front of you, but there may be another, and even another.

We often have many more choices than we realize, including the choice of whether to manage or lead. Managing involves maintaining or enhancing the ability of an enterprise, a noble and important goal, as we've discussed. Leading involves moving to a better future. You choose when to perform which behavior. To make that choice, you have to understand *why* you're making the decision you're making.

How do you know when to choose leadership? When is it worth it to take a risk to lead people into an unknown future? To many people, the "leader" is the person tasked with a big job—for example, the person responsible for opening a new factory. But it doesn't take courage to get people to follow you when they are being paid to do just that. Choosing leadership is harder than being given a big job and doing what you're expected to do, so on what basis do you choose to lead?

To answer that, you need to understand the gist of your motivations. It's possible you'll do every activity in this book and still not have a handle on that; it's an ongoing process and a lifelong activity. As former CEO of GE Jeff Immelt has said, "Leadership is a deep journey into yourself. "

QUESTION

When do you take a risk to change the future?

The Management of Meaning

You'll want to be able to communicate gist once you've found it, and there are a few strategies you can use to do that. One of the most important ways to manage meaning is through the use of symbols.

When I was a young professor at Stanford, Jeff Pfeffer taught me about the importance of managing meaning. Champions manage meaning in many ways, including with words, images, behavior, and awards. You can also do it by highlighting success stories in newsletters, on websites, and in social media, for example. Because things that catch our attention are readily available in our memory, they become emphasized in our decisions. In psychology, this is called the availability bias. Symbols can help you use availability bias to your advantage to capture people's attention and make the gist more salient for them.

Think about awards. At a ceremony, people gather publicly and recognize someone, making salient the value behind or reason for the award. In my executive education classroom, I use a symbol to welcome back previous students who have returned to take another course with me. I give them a small, symbolic gift for returning to my classroom, and I do this to publicly acknowledge the people who found enough value in my teaching to return for more. This is the availability bias in action.

I also created a "whistle-stop" award to make salient another value I want to communicate: that of stopping to consider an alternative course of action. Teachers, including myself, put a lot of hard work into planning our lessons, and once in a classroom, we may be so committed to our lesson plans that we become less focused on the students. Because of this, we sometimes don't have the motivation to stop and change course if the students want to go in a different direction.

Recognizing this default in myself, I created a whistle-stop award to demonstrate to my students that I value their input. The idea is this: When a train travels through the countryside, it has scheduled stops on its route, but it will make an unscheduled stop if a passenger pulls the whistle at the station. When someone pulls the whistle in my class and stops the train to ask a perceptive question, one that is worthy of an unscheduled stop in my classroom, I publicly give that person a wooden train whistle. This is a symbol that shows the students that I am willing to make that stop. And consider the power of a symbol: The whistle only has this particular meaning because I use it to communicate this gist directly. Out of context, it's just a noisy, wooden toy.

Fireside chats or conversations are other ways to manage meaning. So are images or photos. In my classroom, I show a photo of my favorite zigzag bridge, a style of bridge common to Asian gardens. A zigzag bridge typically doesn't have handrails, so you must be mindful when crossing to avoid falling into the water below. I want students to associate that image with the importance of slowing down, being in the moment, and reflecting. In my classroom, I show an image of a zigzag bridge to remind students to take time for individual reflection. This is how an image can be used to manage meaning.

Another symbol that I've seen used is the hat. Recall from the preface that I taught leadership with Howard Haas, the former CEO of Sealy. In class, Howard used to wear a baseball cap to illustrate choice. His management hat was blue with a capital *M*, and he used to explain that it's the hat to wear any time you are working in the present and managing through compliance, legitimate power, reward power, and coercive power. As a manager, you have the authority to ask your employees to do a given task, as well as the power to reward and punish.

Other times he put on a red hat bearing the cursive letter *L*. This was his leadership hat, red to make the point that leadership can be dangerous. When you decide to lead, you are heading into the future toward a place that doesn't yet exist. With that hat on, you have to believe strongly and have confidence in yourself and your vision of a better tomorrow.

At the start of this book, I challenged you to try referring to leading rather than leaders, to use the verb rather than the noun. But we all default to using the word "leader." I'm trying to use a different word here, specifically "champion," substituting another label in order to manage meaning in a conscious, intentional way.

What symbols do you use, in your family perhaps, to communicate gist? Do you present images? Give awards? Use certain words or phrases?

Join Me on the Mezzanine

When communicating gist, it's important to do so in a way that is neither too concrete nor too abstract. We need to get to the *mezzanine*.

When you're in a discussion, you're often talking about something at a level that may be termed concrete. For example, reflect on the story of your earliest leadership experience and why you chose the example you did.

How does the story exemplify your personal take on leadership?

_____

_____

_____

You may have answered this by recounting some of the descriptive details of your story. If Connie were answering, for example, she might point out that she was a mom, at a hotel, who physically pushed past hotel management and sat in her car in the cold and snow. But at this point, what do we learn from this description of her story? Not much. We're stuck in the weeds of concrete details and losing the broader meaning.

She could instead say her story showed that safety is always her highest priority. That may be true, but it's too high-level and abstract to be useful. My favorite example of abstraction is the oft-heard admonition, "We have to align individual and corporate goals." Sure, we can all agree that doing this might be a good idea, but what it actually means, nobody knows. It's not actionable in any practical way. If Connie always places a high value on safety, what does that tell us about her leadership choice? Does it imply that her leadership choices will always be driven by safety, even when safety is not at issue?

To communicate gist, it's important to get to the mezzanine, that sweet spot in a discussion that's above the level of the weeds but below the clouds. On the mezzanine, we have an understanding that can be generalized beyond the current situation. We get the core essence of a concept.

At this sweet spot, what do we learn about Connie? What about her earliest leadership story helps us understand when she takes a stand? In her role as a parent, she was responsible for the physical safety of her children in an apparent emergency. An authority figure told her to do something that went against her concern about a situation and threatened to

CHAPTER 3

undermine her ability to keep her children safe. At that point, she had a choice. The authority figure had both legitimate power and expert power. Compliance would have been the simplest thing to do. But she made the choice to push past this authority figure—in her pajamas, into the night, when it was snowing—and people followed her.

The leadership definition implied by Connie's story involves a strong sense of responsibility, courage in the face of authority, and the presence of followers. Even though it turned out that there was no fire, she selected this story as her earliest leadership experience. It was a case where she stepped up to keep people safe, knowing that she would have to live with the consequences of her decision.

The phrase "join me on the mezzanine" originated with my husband some years ago when we were having a disagreement. I was trying to make him understand my side of an argument by using concrete details from our conversation, but the information was too detailed for him and too directly tied to my viewpoint. In exasperation, he looked at me and asked, "Would you like to join me on the mezzanine, so that we can actually solve this problem?" He was basically saying, "Bring it one level up so we can communicate."

My husband is a professor who does research in communication, so in this example, he was thinking about communicating, while I was thinking about understanding. Although I hate to admit it, he is often correct: we need to both communicate and come to an understanding on the mezzanine. Learn fundamental knowledge at the mezzo level of analysis so that you can apply that knowledge not only to the specific example that you may be dealing with but to other situations, too.

Champions need to get to that sweet spot. We must bring people to the mezzanine.

Mezzanine, Applied

This notion of the mezzanine is central to choosing leadership. You want to be able to take certain fundamental knowledge and apply it to situations that matter to you at three levels of understanding:

1. Individual/Interpersonal	→	Self/Partner
2. Groups/Teams	→	Family
3. Societal/Organizational	→	Community

With an understanding of biases and defaults, you can take your knowledge of gist and apply it at the individual, group, and societal levels.

Think about people who are "normal neurotics," as I call them. These are people who are smart and successful and who go around trying to maintain or enhance their sense of self. You and I are likely normal neurotics. Normal neurotics have common defaults, such as *confirmation bias*, in which we seek to confirm our preferred hypotheses. If I think that I have the right answer to a question, and Nick agrees with me, I conclude that Nick is a pretty smart guy. After all, he has the right answer, too. The same idea expressed at the group level is *groupthink*, group-level confirmation bias. After a group decides about the desired course of action, instead of raising critical questions and seeking disconfirming evidence, it suppresses dissent and looks for evidence that confirms its preferred hypothesis.

Confirmation bias also exists at the organizational or societal level. This bias can be considered *ethnocentrism*. It leads to statements such as, "Our group is good," and, "We're right; they're wrong." In their book *Nudge*, Richard Thaler and Cass Sunstein illustrate how you can apply these understandings at the organizational/societal level to situations of importance to health, wealth, and happiness. In doing so, they identify psychological fundamentals that can be put to use in our lives to make us more productive.

For example, on the mezzanine, we understand how automatic opt-in programs can affect our behavior. If a default is set for you to invest monthly in a retirement account, and you have to take the time to consciously opt out of investing, you are likely to save more for retirement. The realization of how to apply these understandings at the societal level can be profound.

As *Nudge* points out, requiring people to opt out is a type of "nudge." To increase retirement savings, the lesson here is to create a situation where people have to opt out of—not into—a 401k program. People could still choose not to participate, but they would have to put in effort to opt out, and only those people who care a lot about the issue would bother to do that.

On the mezzanine, it's easier to recognize core principles and psychological biases. Learn to observe and work with them at several levels of understanding. The same principles can be applied across various levels if you understand the gist.

> When we create our own structures, and reduce our reliance on externally provided ones, we increase our ability to handle ambiguity.

From the mezzanine, you can also get more perspective on the use of labels. Just as I prefer the label "champion" over the labels "managers" and "leaders," Harold Leavitt liked the hybrid label "manager-leader." Instead of focusing on the words themselves, move to the mezzanine and think about the fundamental principle underlying what each of us is saying. We're all trying to think more productively about what it means to both lead and manage.

Commencement Speeches

Here's another exercise that will help you get to and communicate gist. In your *This I Believe* essay (Activity 3.1, page 50), you had to distill and communicate gist in 350–500 words. Now the goal is to write a commencement speech, where you will do something similar in eleven minutes.

While both exercises require analyzing and editing, there is an important difference between them: your essay conveyed your personal credo, but a commencement speech conveys what you feel is important for other people to know. All eyes may be on you, but your speech is not about you; it is about the graduates listening to the speech. What do you want them to know? I've written here that it is important to pay special attention to beginnings and endings, and a commencement speech is both. It's simultaneously the end of students' educations and the beginning of their lives beyond the classroom.

What would you say in a commencement speech? What wisdom do you think is worthy of your speech? It's a great exercise that requires discipline.

ACTIVITY 3.2 Your Commencement Speech

Try writing a commencement speech of your own. As with other activities, I encourage you to work on it now and revisit it periodically in the future. Before you start, read excerpts of a few tips from the website of Tony Balis, founder of the nonprofit Humanity Initiative, on how to write a profound, inspirational speech.

1. **HONOR THE OCCASION:** Make it about their lives, not yours. . . . Most speakers inherently "get" that a commencement is an intimate occasion, not a public one. The best speakers understand that they therefore are deeply responsible to their audience. Your challenge is to memorialize the occasion with as compelling and inspiring a message as you can muster, avoiding the lethal temptations of political persuasion, of complacency, or of an unrestrained ego.

2. **KEEP IT UNDER EIGHTEEN MINUTES:** Cut. Edit. Chop. Delete. Do the hard work of being precise.

3. **BE UTTERLY YOURSELF:** Know what you are saying. Feel it in your heart more than your head, for that's where the graduates will hear you best. Emotional honesty works well in any speech. . . . Say what you know and what is truly important to you.

4. **STARTLE THEM:** As you are being introduced, the graduates, understandably, are distracted by many different things, most having nothing to do with you. You need to startle them, to command their attention.

Use the space provided on the following page to begin drafting your speech. For inspiration, I recommend that you read *10 1/2 Things No Commencement Speaker Has Ever Said*, by Charles Wheelan.

ACTIVITY 3.2 Your Commencement Speech (continued)

Skyscrapers and Leadership

For group learning, use Leadership Module 3.C: Structural Integrity (15 minutes)

I know firsthand how tough it is to write a commencement speech and to communicate the core essence in your message. I was invited to speak at the 86th Executive MBA Graduation Ceremony at Chicago Booth in 2017, and here's the gist of what I said: The sky is the limit for people once we look less to external reference points for strength and work on building our inner core. I saw a parallel in architecture, where pioneers shed "load bearing assumptions" to build skyscrapers. Similarly, building a stronger internal framework helps us to have the courage to choose leadership. Here is an essay based on my speech:

> In 1872, a twenty-eight-year-old apprentice draftsman named Daniel Burnham opened an architecture firm with his good friend, John Root. Burnham and Root would soon become one of the finest architectural firms in this city.
>
> Among the firm's best work is the Monadnock Building, in Chicago's Loop, at the corner of Dearborn and Jackson. If you have time, or when you tour Chicago, I hope that you will see this building. There's a very good coffee shop, and a hat shop, and a great, old shoe-repair business. If you go to visit, pay particular attention to the walls. They are 6 feet thick, almost 2 meters, at the base. They had to be that wide to support the weight of the 16-story-high building.
>
> For thousands of years, buildings had to have thick walls because the walls carried the weight of the entire structure. The higher the building, the thicker the walls had to be. The Monadnock Building represented an amazing architectural achievement: it was the tallest load-bearing building ever built, and it was the tallest office building in the world. John Root called this building his "Jumbo." It was his last project because he died suddenly of pneumonia while it was under construction.

But the Monadnock Building was a great achievement that also represented the limits of an age-old concept. It made sense that the walls had to be heavy and strong in order to hold the weight of the building. But with load-bearing walls, a building can only go so high. As the ambitions of city planners and residents rose, so did the desires of architects and their clients to build even higher. But how could you build a really, really tall building without building really, really thick walls?

A man named William Le Baron Jenney came up with the answer. Jenney is widely recognized as the father of the American skyscraper, and according to Chicago lore, he had a breakthrough idea when he observed his wife placing a very heavy book on top of a tall metal birdcage. The cage not only supported the weight of the book, Jenney could see that it could have easily supported a whole stack of books. A stack of books piled high and balancing on a birdcage—what an image.

Jenney introduced the idea of a complete steel skeleton, and he built the first fully metal-framed skyscraper in Chicago in 1884. Just as his wife had used a birdcage to support the weight of a very big book, Jenney used metal columns and beams to support his building from the inside.

With Jenney's new framework, limits on the height of buildings changed. Walls became more like hanging curtains made of glass, and columns within the buildings bore the structure's weight across the foundation. Buildings began rising to impressive new heights, and together with the development of plumbing, electricity, and elevators, and most importantly with the invention of the elevator braking system, the sky was literally the limit.

If you go to the top of the Willis Tower (the old Sears Tower) or any other famous skyscraper on a tour of Chicago, you will see much more than an extraordinary view. You will see the power of abandoning long-held assumptions.

The assumption that walls held up a building dominated for many years and limited architects' progress. Their load-bearing assumptions quite literally served as an upper boundary to the height of the buildings they could design. Jenney's vision to use metal-frame-core construction was brilliant. It represented a completely new way of thinking about the source of strength—the strength of an inner framework. This story demonstrates the combined power of shedding a default assumption that weighed people down with making a major conceptual shift, which, in this case, provided architects the strength they needed to build higher.

Many of us face load-bearing assumptions, perhaps about management, strategy, finance, or leadership. For example, you may assume that the economic world is a zero-sum game. Or that some people can systematically beat the market without any inside information. Or that debt is a cheaper form of finance because it is less risky. Or that issuing equity is bad because it dilutes earnings. You may even assume that some people are natural-born leaders while others are not, as opposed to holding the view that leadership is a choice.

Shedding assumptions is not an easy task because many have served you well in the past, and there is risk in abandoning them. Yet one of the most important skills that you can acquire is a willingness to question your load-bearing assumptions and make a different choice, when necessary.

Now, there is a second thing that is important for you to notice about skyscrapers. In my classroom, we speak often about the frameworks that allow us to think more complexly about business issues across industries, economics, and geographies. When I teach leadership, I emphasize building our own personal frameworks. When we create our own structures and reduce our reliance on externally provided ones, we increase our ability to handle ambiguity. Creating our own frameworks can help us to be wiser, younger, and to learn more from everyday experience—and what we learn can better inform our choices. Just as a skyscraper's strength comes from its core, the clarity, vision, and support for your own framework must come from your core. There is no blueprint for your future.

In architecture, structural integrity is established during the planning phase and built into the foundation. William Le Baron Jenney taught us to build up by building from within. You need that same kind of structural integrity. Build from within. Build your frame with strong values. Build with unselfishness, kindness, and curiosity. Build with open-mindedness to new ideas, with compassion, and with a sense of fairness. Your own inner framework will determine how high you can go. I hope you will continue to rise above your load-bearing assumptions, and keep building a strong, inner framework to ensure the integrity of all you do.

> **Education is not preparation for life; education is life itself.** —JOHN DEWEY

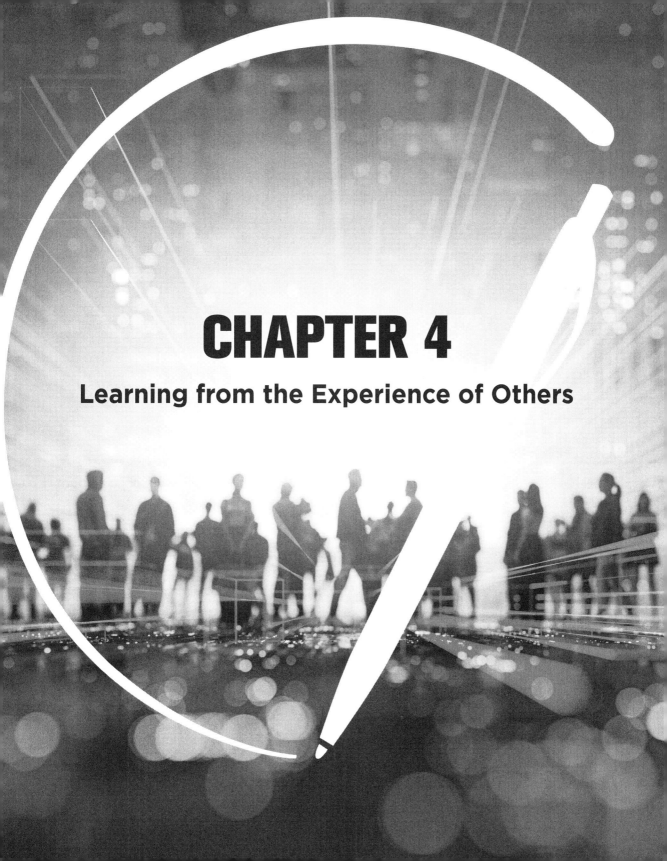

CHAPTER 4

Learning from the Experience of Others

You should now have a basic understanding of gist, and this will be the foundation of your work going forward. There are at least two ways to learn from experience. We'll focus first on how to learn from others' experiences, before turning in the next chapter to how to learn from our own experiences.

Because we are constantly bombarded by others' happenings, there is a lot of opportunity for learning from interviews, speeches, movies, TED Talks, books, and such things. The good news for a student of leadership is that you can turn just about anything into a personal development activity. And you can become wiser, younger by vicariously learning lessons from others. Books, movies, and various summaries of other people's experiences can help you identify and understand themes that are important to you. You can use these summaries to better understand your own past decisions, access your sense of purpose, and identify the enduring values that guide your choices.

Here's more good news: You already know how to learn from others because you learned this as a child. Children learn almost everything they know from modeling, that is, looking at and copying other people's behaviors. But sometimes adults forget how to engage in vicarious learning, so here is an exercise designed to help you get back to that.

To learn from observation, you have to be able to integrate what you take in with your own understanding of things. Speeches, books, and other summaries provide raw data, and you need a way of deciding what is uniquely important to you. A framework can help you customize your learning by helping you take your own context into account. It can help you extract value from things, but first, of course, you have to create your own frameworks.

Knowledge is abstract, raw data is messy, and information is mostly unstructured. We have to figure out how to collect, organize, and process it. Ultimately, we have to create a structure; a way of organizing knowledge and data for action. If this description of frameworks sounds at all vague, that's because there is no one "correct" format for a framework. Some use only text, while others incorporate images, tables, or diagrams. A framework might be a spreadsheet, a paragraph, a flowchart, a drawing, or something else entirely. Your framework could be completely different from someone else's but just as effective for your own purpose.

ACTIVITY 4.1 Vicarious Learning Framework

In this exercise, draft a framework for vicarious learning. This framework should outline a systematic way for you to collect data that can be analyzed and acted upon. The structure you create will help you to reduce the ambiguity that could otherwise inhibit your progress. Consider what might be most useful to you, including focus, scope, and format or structure. As you create your "zero draft," remember not only to consider what lessons are important for you to learn but also to speculate about how your future self might act upon these insights.

This vicarious learning framework is a draft for you to develop as you continue to learn the lessons of others' experience. Continue refining and editing your framework. Revisit this draft and update it to address ongoing challenges.

ACTIVITY 4.1 Vicarious Learning Framework (continued)

Organizing Frameworks

For group learning, use Leadership Module 4.A: Vicarious Learning (20 Minutes)

Frameworks represent structure. It's something that exists to organize and impose order on data so that you can process it. The ability to handle ambiguity is among the most sought-after skills in executives. When a global executive search firm recently hired one of my former students, the recruiter told her that the ability to handle ambiguity is "what all the firms are looking for."

This made me think more about how to help champions to function in a state of ambiguity, given the comfort that comes with closure. Resolving ambiguity is also something that groups must do in order to find clarity and reach consensus. In a classroom, professors provide ready-made frameworks to use while diagnosing case studies and applying theories. But outside the classroom, you don't have those ready-made structures provided to you. It's up to you to figure out how to handle real-world ambiguity. This is why it's important to learn to build your own frameworks. Creating your own structure will help you learn more from everyday experience and guide your future choices. You'll reduce your reliance on externally provided guidelines and increase your ability to handle ambiguity.

Several activities in this book will give you the opportunity to practice designing frameworks. The goal is for the structures you create to be flexible and generalizable so you can use them in different situations that you might encounter in the future. As with all activities in this book, these are meant to be customized by you and to serve as a vehicle for your ongoing self-development.

Think about the data presented in your vicarious-learning framework. How did you organize it? How did your structure highlight what is most important? How will it help you to move toward action? How quickly can you look at your framework and make sense of the data? What manner of organizing and structuring your thoughts will best help you to analyze situations and make decisions in various aspects of your life? These questions can help you tease out important attributes of the frameworks you design.

This table is an example of one vicarious-learning framework. It was provided by Edny Inui, a former student who created it to help her collect and organize data from guest speakers. Her goal was to both learn from the various speakers and develop her network of future contacts.

Table 4.1: **SPA Vicarious-Learning Framework**

Name:

Education [circle if in network]:

Current position:

Previous relevant positions:

Potential question/Question asked:

Title [or theme]:

Context [one-on-one, roundtable, conference]:

STYLE: What stands out about this person's personal style that was unique or compelling?

SUCCESS: What was the key to this person's success?

PITFALLS: How did this person overcome a tough situation?

PITHY: Impact/Direct quote [I collect compelling quotes to use in my thought leadership pieces and for personal inspiration]

ACTION: Did this talk inspire me or remind me to do something?

ACCOUNTABILITY: In what timeframe should I complete this action?

What were three key takeaways from this talk:

1. _____

2. _____

3. _____

How likely would I be to reach out to this person in the future: LEAST 1 2 3 4 5 6 7 8 9 10 MOST

How likely would they be to respond: LEAST 1 2 3 4 5 6 7 8 9 10 MOST

What would be the purpose of the contact?

_____

Special contact notes [email, phone, instructions]:

_____

Public Lectures and Speeches

What kind of situation would call for you to use a vicarious-learning framework? Think about some of the ways people summarize, distill, and present their experiences. TED Talks are one example. TED founder Chris Anderson said that his idea was to invite the best and the brightest to "give the greatest talk of their lives" in eighteen minutes. These talks, available free of charge as online videos, are among the most engaging public lectures available. My sentimental favorite is Harvard's Daniel Gilbert on the surprising science of happiness. Why not watch Dan's talk with others and discuss what each member of your group considers the gist?

For group learning, use Leadership Module 4.B: Lectures and Speeches (30 Minutes)

When you watch a TED Talk, digest what's presented in terms of your own behavior. Look for general patterns in your own life. Integrate the content coming at you with your experiences and unique interpretation. Only you know what speaks to you; there are lots of ways to construct frameworks to extract value from a public lecture, but what framework best enables you to capture the value you seek from any given experience? Here are a few activities to get you experimenting with frameworks and thinking more complexly.

> If you are interested in learning more about the social psychology of happiness, be sure to read Dan Gilbert's book *Stumbling on Happiness.*

Make Your Own Top 10 Framework

When David Letterman was on the air, he had a regular segment on late-night television where he read a list of 10 items relating to a single theme, capping the end of the reverse countdown with a drumroll. They were meant to be humorous, with titles such as "The top 10 children's books not recommended by the National Library Association." When I teach negotiations, my students recap the course with a Top 10 list of their own. Their lists are incredibly funny and creatively capture their favorite lessons with titles such as "Top 10 things never to say in a negotiation," or "Top 10 emails Professor Ginzel does not want to receive."

Next time you have the opportunity to listen to a speech or lecture, practice making your own Top 10 list.

ACTIVITY 4.2 Your "Top 10" Framework

10. _____

_____

9. _____

_____

8. _____

_____

7. _____

_____

6. _____

_____

5. _____

_____

4. _____

_____

3. _____

_____

2. _____

_____

1. _____

_____

CHOOSING LEADERSHIP

After one of my favorite executives, Uptake's Sonny Garg, was a visiting lecturer in my leadership class, I created this Top 10 list:

TOP 10 LESSONS FROM SONNY GARG

10. Read the "Letter from Birmingham Jail" by Martin Luther King Jr.

9. Management is the most noble of professions if it's practiced well.

8. The hardest thing to do is to get work done through others.

7. You can't do something differently if you don't change your behavior.

6. Our lives are driven by the "hows," not the "whys." We jump to the "how," but if you don't take time to figure out the "why," you can't get it done.

5. Organizations don't resist change. People resist the change that they are not a part of.

4. "Once I made you rich enough, rich enough to forget my name." —Bruce Springsteen, from "Youngstown"

3. Treating people with respect and dignity is important for sustainable change.

2. You never want to bring anyone into the conversation if you aren't interested in listening.

1. If you have a choice between reading a business book and great fiction, read more literature.

You could make other Top 10 lists. For example, if you collect quotes, how might you rank your Top 10 favorite quotes? Here is a quote mentioned by Sonny:

"I would not give a fig for the simplicity this side of complexity, but I would give my life for the simplicity on the other side of complexity." —Oliver Wendell Holmes Jr.

One of Sonny's lessons is to learn more from things around you. In fact, my number-one lesson from him is "read more literature." Similarly, Harvard's Joseph L. Badaracco Jr. recommends learning from leaders featured in fiction:

> Serious fiction suggests that leaders should learn more about themselves if they want to succeed . . . You should reflect on how well you can manage yourself. That takes time, and it is an unnatural act for action-oriented people. And you may not like what you see. But if Sophocles teaches us that leaders cannot escape their flawed humanity, he also suggests that we can lower the risks of error and tragedy though sound reflection.

Let Badaracco inspire you, and try learning from Sophocles. In his teaching of leadership, Howard Haas would always recommend Hermann Hesse's *The Journey to the East*. If you want to tackle other great literature, there's always Shakespeare. One of my favorites is *Henry V*, but there is also *King Lear* and *Othello* and plenty more wisdom to be found in most everything he wrote.

My Booth colleague Harry Davis introduced me to *The Alchemist* by Paulo Coelho when we first started teaching together. He uses it to help executives explore the metaphor of journey. The young protagonist, Santiago, goes off in search of treasure and learns many life lessons along the way. It is a story that can be understood differently at different times in your life—especially when you're at a crossroads and need help deciding which path to take.

Leadership at the Movies

For group learning, use Leadership Module 4.C: Leadership at the Movies (30 Minutes)

Learning can be as simple as going to the movies, as films provide another way to learn by observation. There are many film critics who can guide you in selecting great films. To make "Leadership at the Movies" a family activity, my recommendation is Nell Minow's *The Movie Mom's Guide to Family Movies*.

Three of my favorite films that can aid your leadership development are *Rashomon*, *Invictus*, and *Temple Grandin*. To get in the right frame of mind, if you happen to be near your computer, google "Reel Wisdom: Lessons from 40 Films in 7 Minutes." It's a great clip of pithy lessons. Then, when you have time for a movie, screen one of these three. Watch the movie, then answer the questions included on the next page to help you think deeply about the leadership themes at hand and capture your personal gist.

> Our mission was called 'a successful failure' in that we returned safely, but never made it to the Moon.
>
> —JAMES LOVELL, FROM THE MOVIE *APOLLO 13*

Rashomon

This 1950 film takes place in twelfth-century Japan. A bandit kills a samurai and rapes the samurai's wife. The bandit is captured shortly afterward, but his version of what happened differs from the accounts of the wife and the deceased samurai, who gives his own testimony through a psychic. A woodcutter who finds the body reveals that he saw the whole thing, and his version is completely different from the others. The film gives four viewpoints of the same incident, with each revealing a different perspective.

While watching, focus on assessing what motivates each of the characters to tell a different story of the tragic incident.

- "It is human to lie. Most of the time we cannot even be honest with ourselves." —Commoner

- "I'm the one who should be ashamed. I don't understand my own soul." —Woodcutter

- "Dead men tell no lies." —Priest

When you struggle with difficult issues requiring introspection, such as those in *Rashomon*, it is often helpful to go to the mezzanine. Here are some questions to help you get to your gist of this movie:

? QUESTIONS

1. What is the hard truth?

_____

_____

_____

_____

2. What motivates people to tell a different story?

_____

_____

_____

_____

3. What are the stories that I choose to tell about who I am?

_____

_____

_____

_____

4. What do each of the characters help us understand about identity?

_____

_____

_____

_____

Invictus

In this 2009 film based on John Carlin's 2008 book, *Playing the Enemy*, Nelson Mandela recounts how he worked to end apartheid and fought for the right to vote. After being released from Robben Island prison after twenty-seven years, he won election as president of South Africa. Mandela came to power at a time when his country was racially and economically divided. He worked to unite his apartheid-torn country by enlisting the national rugby team on a mission to win the 1995 Rugby World Cup.

While watching the film, consider how the rugby team is a symbol of this divided nation.

QUESTIONS

1. Where do you go to find inspiration?

2. How do you know if you are making the right change?

3. How do you determine the amount of risk to take in choosing leadership?

4. When have you exceeded your expectations?

_____

_____

_____

_____

5. How has adversity moved you?

_____

_____

_____

Of course, just as you can learn from movies and literature, you can learn from poetry. This is the 1888 poem written by William Ernest Henley that Mandela said gave him strength when he was in jail.

> "Invictus"
>
> Out of the night that covers me,
>
> Black as the pit from pole to pole,
>
> I thank whatever gods may be
>
> For my unconquerable soul.
>
> In the fell clutch of circumstance
>
> I have not winced nor cried aloud.
>
> Under the bludgeonings of chance
>
> My head is bloody, but unbowed.
>
> Beyond this place of wrath and tears

Looms but the Horror of the shade,

And yet the menace of the years

Finds and shall find me unafraid.

It matters not how strait the gate,

How charged with punishments the scroll,

I am the master of my fate,

I am the captain of my soul.

> **?** QUESTION
> What is the gist of this poem for you?

_____

_____

_____

_____

_____

Temple Grandin

This film pick was suggested to me by Randy Lewis, a former Walgreens executive. Claire Danes plays Temple Grandin, an autistic woman who changed the cattle industry by creating a new method for humane slaughter. Grandin thinks differently than many of her colleagues. She has enormous capacity, despite stereotypes many people have about people on the autism spectrum. Today she is a professor of animal science at Colorado State University. This movie can challenge what you think about capacity or the scope of what one can accomplish and what it means to improve outcomes across time and place.

While watching the film, think about the challenges Temple Grandin had to overcome.

1. What did the various people in her life (e.g., Temple's mother, aunt, and science teacher) do to cultivate her strengths?

_____

_____

_____

_____

2. When she was trying to convince the slaughterhouse to adopt her idea, what was her most successful tactic? Why did they ultimately listen to her?

_____

_____

_____

3. What were some of the challenges she faced at the slaughterhouse when trying to get them to adopt her design? What could management have done to be more supportive?

_____

_____

_____

4. How might you cultivate someone who doesn't quite fit the mold?

_____

_____

_____

In the movie, during her graduation ceremony, Grandin says, "Today, more than ever, I realize that I have not walked alone. And I thank not only my teachers, but my friends and family as well." Her words spoke to me, and I took them as a jumping off point to create the framework below. Consider how people in your family, schools, communities, and workplaces have affected you and shaped your identity.

After watching the movie about Grandin, you might enjoy seeing and hearing from the real Temple Grandin herself. She gave a TED Talk, "The World Needs All Kinds of Minds," which is available online. And, just like you, Temple Grandin also wrote her own This I Believe essay, which is available on the show's website. If you are interested in learning more, she also wrote a book, *The Way I See It: A Personal Look at Autism and Asperger's.*

ACTIVITY 4.3 "I have not walked alone" Framework

List the significant people in your life from each category below:

1. Family and friends

_____   _____

_____   _____

2. Teachers

_____   _____

_____   _____

3. Professional contacts

_____   _____

_____   _____

4. Community (e.g., religious leader)

_____   _____

_____   _____

ACTIVITY 4.3 "I have not walked alone" Framework (continued)

5. Public figures (e.g., historical)

_____   _____
_____   _____
_____   _____

6. Other

_____   _____
_____   _____
_____   _____

Analysis

Why have each of the people you listed had such an impact on you?

_____
_____
_____

What have you learned about choosing leadership from each?

_____
_____
_____

Action

How might you use the lessons learned from each of these people to inform your future self?

How would you thank these people—past and present—for the influences that they have had on your life? Have you already done so?

_____
_____
_____

What would you say to each of them? There is no time like the present to let them know.

_____

_____

_____

Interviewing Like a Reporter

Another important way to learn from others' experiences is through interviewing. As with all types of vicarious learning, interviewing has the significant advantage of benefiting from the lessons of others' failures without suffering any of the negative consequences.

What are the names of three people whom you would most love to interview?

1. _____

2. _____

3. _____

Table 4.2 on the next page contains interviewing advice from my favorite *New York Times* bestselling author, Jonathan Eig. I also recommend that you read the biography, *Ali, a Life*. Jonathan conducted over 500 interviews to tell the life story of Muhammad Ali.

Finally, here's one more expert interviewer you can learn from. Terry Gross hosts the National Public Radio program *Fresh Air*. She is a master interviewer who draws illuminating stories from people she, in many cases, has never met. *The New York Times Magazine* once described her as having "the status of national interviewer. Think of it as a symbolic role, like the poet laureate—someone whose job it is to ask the questions, with a degree of art and honor."

If you don't already listen to *Fresh Air*, you can find it on your local public radio channel or as a podcast. Gross also wrote a book, *All I Did Was Ask: Conversations with Writers, Actors, Musicians, and Artists*. As you read and listen, think about what you can learn from interviewing people.

Table 4.2: Jonathan Eig's Interview Advice

TOP 10 INTERVIEW RULES

1. Be prepared, but don't show it.

2. Choose the right location.

3. Shut up and listen.

4. Ask questions; don't make statements.

5. Don't explain or add to your question.

6. Embrace the awkward pause.

7. Don't try to be smart. Let your subject explain what you don't know.

8. Be bland. Don't try to impress your interview with your personality.

9. Don't be afraid to ask for what you need. Pull back the curtain.

10. Look around.

GREAT QUESTIONS:	GOOD QUESTIONS:	BAD QUESTIONS:
Why?	Who?	Were you angry?
What?	When?	Were you scared?
How?	Where?	Were you surprised?
What do you mean?		Were you disappointed?
Really?		
Hmm.		
Can you say more about that?		
Can you give me an example?		
Tell me about...		

TRY THIS...	NOT THAT
How did it feel getting attacked?	Were you scared when you were attacked?
What was your biggest mistake?	Do you consider that incident a mistake?
How do you feel about your job?	Do you like your job?

What's the Best Advice You've Ever Received?

If you're looking for a single question to ask someone, here's one that elicits useful answers: What's the best advice you ever received? The best advice that I ever received came from Jeff Pfeffer. In 1989, I had moved across the country and gone from single to married, from graduate student to assistant professor, from studying experimental social psychology to teaching organizational behavior, in just one year. I had many demands on my time and not enough energy to get through my day. "When does this all end?" I had asked my beloved dissertation advisor, the late Ned Jones. "What do you mean when does it end? It ends when you die," he replied.

I had clearly asked the wrong question. One day, when Jeff stopped by my office, I told him that I had too many amazing opportunities—to work with people and on projects, to teach, and to present at conferences. "Linda, beware of once-in-a lifetime opportunities that come along every day," he said. Since then, whenever I have found myself becoming anxious about doing too much, and not doing it all very well, I have remembered Jeff's advice. It reminds me that I am the only one who can determine my own priorities.

Fortune magazine once asked Booth's Eugene Fama, a Nobel Prize-winning economist and all-around good guy, for the best advice he ever got. His answer:

> When I came to the University of Chicago in 1960, I was exposed to professors who were involved in the nascent subject of finance, which didn't exist as a discipline at the time. It was all being born, and it just happened that I had come to the place where that birth was happening. So I kind of got into it because everybody there was interested in it.
>
> In my first year I took an intermediate statistics class with a professor named Harry Roberts. I was twenty-one at the time. He was very much like me—he was into all kinds of sports, and he was a runner. I had done a lot of statistics work as an undergraduate and had already worked with data, so I was pretty advanced when I started. But what I learned from Harry was a philosophy. He gave me an attitude toward statistics that has stuck with me ever since.
>
> With formal statistics, you say something—a hypothesis—and then you test it. Harry always said that your criterion

should be not whether you can reject or accept the hypothesis, but what you can learn from the data. The best thing you can do is use the data to enhance your description of the world.

That has been the guiding light of my research. You should use market data to understand markets better, not to say this or that hypothesis is literally true or false. No model is ever strictly true. The real criterion should be: Do I know more about markets when I'm finished than I did when I started? Harry's lesson is one that I've passed on to my students over the forty-nine years that I've been a teacher.

ACTIVITY 4.4 The Best Advice

What's the best advice you ever received? Write your answer here:

Ask this question of someone else and continue to build collective wisdom.

The answer to the question, "What's the best advice you ever received?" can contain useful insight. But it can also kick off an interesting conversation or train of thought. Consider the best advice submitted by one of my former students, which was given by my Booth colleague Scott Meadow:

> Toward the end of my class in private equity during the summer electives, Professor Meadow gave one of his charismatic speeches. The topic was about the pros and cons of getting a job in private equity and contrasting that career path with entrepreneurship and other endeavors. There was one sentence that struck me: "There's this idea, you know, of trying to keep up with the Joneses, and I'm telling you, you'll never succeed and just end up being unhappy and unfulfilled in the long run."

I sent this to Scott Meadow and told him, "I consider this quote from you as evidence—hard data—that it is the 'soft' stuff that matters!"

And he agreed, saying, "In the end, you are so right . . . . I wish I had had more access to soft stuff during my life." I reminded Scott that he still has time to "access soft stuff." His life is not over. And this is precisely what I hope you take away from this chapter.

There's a lot out there to learn from, and much of it is "soft." The soft stuff *is* hard. The typical "hard" science is built on mathematics expressed in equations and models. What makes soft stuff hard is that we don't find the answers we seek in those equations. Leadership can't be derived from numbers alone. It's a deeply human process.

For the remainder of your days, you will continue to have opportunities to be wiser, younger. It doesn't matter how old you are now, or how old you are, ever. As long as you're alive, you will have the opportunity to choose leadership. You continue to have access to the soft stuff and to learn from it. Every talk, book, movie, or conversation presents an opportunity to grow. Embrace this challenge and this outlook. The world is your classroom, and you can be your own teacher.

For group learning, use Leadership Module 4.D: Best Advice (15 Minutes)

CHAPTER 5

Learning from Our Own Experience

Frameworks enable learning from others' experiences, providing you with the structure needed to use books, movies, and other sources to inform your understanding of yourself. But you can only learn from observation when you integrate what you're learning from others with your own understanding. That's why this chapter is focused on how you can learn more from your own experiences.

As we turn to this, think again about your own leadership experiences. In Activity 5.1, write about your most recent leadership experience.

For group learning, use Leadership Module 5: A Recent Leadership Story (15 Minutes)

ACTIVITY 5.1 Your Most Recent Leadership Experience

Is there a common thread that runs between what you chose as one of your earliest leadership experiences in Activity 1.1 and your most recent? Take some time to reflect in order to identify the underlying theme. What is the enduring value that emboldens you to step up and choose leadership?

_____

_____

_____

_____

Here's an example of a thread running through one person's earliest and most recent leadership experiences, as told by Concepción, a former student:

> On the first day of Professor Ginzel's Leadership Capital course, we did an exercise that asked each of us to tell a partner we were sitting next to about our first leadership experience. After my partner told me her first leadership experience, I told her mine. I explained that as a child, I had fully accepted the responsibility of taking care of my younger siblings and being an active contributor to the family. It's a normal thing in Mexican families, especially immigrant families, so I never questioned it and never complained. My portion of helping was taking the role of "big sister," which included driving at a very young age (younger than is legal in the US) to take siblings to school, Mom to run errands like grocery shopping, and the younger ones to their appointments. I was better suited to do these tasks than my mother because she did not speak English or drive, and her hands were full managing seven children, the in-laws, and a revolving door of relatives migrating to Chicago. I spoke English and stepped up to drive and help resolve any obstacles in our routine life in Chicago. I actually enjoyed being a contributor

to the family, taking part in problem solving, and being a role model to my younger siblings.

After the exercise was over, Professor Ginzel asked us to try to find the thread between that first leadership experience and our current situations. It clicked for me in an instant. I am a management consultant because I am accustomed to being the problem solver. Through consulting, I set out to find solutions for my clients and service their needs by implementing change and then supporting their staffs through the transition. It's work that I enjoy very much because I am good at it, having the self-confidence and communication skills to work with many different types of people. I have been serving others most of my professional life, and I recognize I built the expertise by serving my large immigrant family with its variety of personalities and colorful challenges. Furthermore, I manage my own consulting firm. I am an entrepreneur because I like being independent and fully accountable for my own life. In my professional work, I guide my clients through business transformations. In my household, I support my daughters through their days of school, activities, and goals for their futures. I service my clients with as much dedication as I serve my girls. The thread of my first leadership experience to today is service. Being serviceable, useful, and making a difference in people's lives is important to my success.

These stories are among the *punctuation points* of our lives. Punctuation points are defining moments that can serve as vehicles for self-inquiry and self-understanding. According to Joseph Badaracco, among others, such defining moments typically involve a choice between two different paths, one of which ends up shaping our characters and revealing our underlying values.

The late Warren G. Bennis, a pioneer of leadership studies, wrote in his book *On Becoming a Leader* about points of self-reflection, describing them as experiences that force you to ask deep, existential questions about identity and meaning. He refers to these experiences as crucibles, after the vessels medieval alchemists used while trying to turn metal into gold. A crucible is also a severe test or trial that causes a lasting change or influence. Bennis, together with Robert J. Thomas in their book *Leading for a Lifetime,* further explored the idea that such experiences have a lasting influence.

For group learning, use Leadership Module 5.B: Life Lessons (30 Minutes)

 QUESTION
What defining moments or crucible experiences have pushed you outside your comfort zone?

_____

_____

_____

Many authors talk about these punctuation points as negative events that are forced upon us, and therefore are out of our control. However, positive experiences, including those that we choose for ourselves, can also shape who we become. Social psychology teaches that if you want to change your identity, you start by changing your behavior. This is similar to some words of wisdom one of my students told me that he received from his father: "First you choose your habits, and then they choose you." This is the logic that underlies your next activity, which will require you to look back to your past and forward to your future self.

We are what we repeatedly do. Excellence, then, is not an act, but a habit. —ARISTOTLE

 QUESTION
In this chapter, you will revisit moments that shaped your life. What would you say if someone asked about your biggest influence? Complete this sentence:

I wouldn't be here now if . . .

_____

_____

_____

_____

Identifying your biggest influence is a first step. The next step, when choosing leadership, is to link insight to action. Knowledge is necessary but insufficient. How do you process that knowledge, and what do you decide to do with the insights you gain?

Here's one such action implication: Have you told the person whose name you wrote here about the profound effect that he or she has had on your life? If not, this could be your first action step. Activity 5.2 will help you identify and learn from your punctuation points.

ACTIVITY 5.2 Lifelines, Past and Future Selves

1. Draw a line on a sheet of paper that begins with your first memory and ends with today.

2. Draw another line that begins with today and ends ten, twenty, or thirty-plus years from now.

3. Identify the major punctuation points that have shaped who you are, and anticipate the points that you hope will shape your future self.

4. Reflect on those defining moments to better understand why you marked them as important. Were these moments in your past expected and planned, or were they unexpected and unplanned? Did they involve success or failure? What are those punctuation points you hope to create for your future self, and how?

_____

_____

_____

_____

Your Life Story

In the previous chapter, we explored what you can learn about leadership at the movies. Here's an idea from the 2000 movie *High Fidelity*. John Cusack plays a record-store owner, Rob Gordon, who tells the story of his life in terms of his top-five romantic breakups. Rob's huge record collection is also organized autobiographically by periods in his life. This is another framework for thinking about the punctuation points of your life.

If you are a music lover, you might love the idea of organizing your life story in terms of record albums. But different approaches work for different people. What theme is meaningful to you in summarizing different periods of your life? Try it here by summarizing your life story in terms of the top five events that have led you to where you are now.

1. _____

2. _____

3. _____

4. _____

5. _____

In *The 7 Habits of Highly Effective People*, Stephen Covey wrote that one of these habits was to "start with the end in mind." There are a variety of ways you can process this bit of wisdom and make it your own, but perhaps the most direct way is to write your own obituary. By starting with the end of your life in mind, you can think about how you want to live your life moving forward. (If you are interested in this activity and want more inspiration, there's a lot of advice online about how to write your own obituary.)

I have been moved to learn from my own experiences by people who, knowing their end was near, have written books and recorded videos as part of the legacies they wanted to leave for their young children and other loved ones. The heart-wrenching, soul-searching *When Breath Becomes Air*, by the neurosurgeon Paul Kalanithi, is one such book. Another is *The Last Lecture* by Randy Pausch, who was a professor at Carnegie Mellon. It is available as a book, but I suggest that you also watch the lecture, available on YouTube. You likely have many more years ahead of you, but the stories of these two insightful people can still serve as examples of how to be deeply reflective.

Leadership Role Models

Much of what you learn through observation is from the experiences of people you know, whether from home, work, or your community. But you also learn by observing people you don't know personally but only by reputation.

In general, I do not like to use business leaders as exemplars because doing so contributes to a hero worship that I believe to be detrimental to the professional development of champions and the outcomes of their organizations. That said, it can be helpful in choosing leadership to look to role models—both positive and negative—in government, industry, media, history, and literature, as well as to other public figures. Positive role models are people you look to and say, "I want to be like her." With negative role models, you say, "I never want to be like her."

Here are two more leadership stories to illustrate the power of negative and positive role models in our lives. This one is from a former student named Joe:

> In the movie *Inception,* Leonardo DiCaprio and his team have the seemingly impossible task of implanting another person's idea into the target's subconscious. About 10 years into my job, my new manager (let's call him Tom) did just that for me with an idea. Always treat people with respect and dignity because no matter how many life-changing management lessons I learned from Tom, the greatest lasting impression was how he treated others.
>
> When I became a new line manager, a multi-million dollar project was given to me to lead as well as to manage, and

CHAPTER 5

to develop direct reports ranging [in age] from twenty-five years old to fifty years old. And I had zero management experience. From day one, I "drank from a fire hose" on leading the project and people. Every week, I brought a slew of questions to Tom. What do I say when direct report "A" brings a concern or a problem about this or that process? How do I say it? When do I say it? There were many lessons that were instilled in me from his feedback. One that I still remember is that bringing a problem without a solution is a complaint. Another feedback was that we're here to do a job and complainers can be replaced. There are 100 people out there who would be grateful to have this job. Both lessons and feedback left an imprint and memory in my life. However, the lasting imprint was that I was able to immediately recall the complainer comment versus having to think for several minutes to recall the valuable management lesson about bringing a solution. Overall, this was Tom's leadership philosophy. Although he rewarded people for their contributions, Tom treated people as if they were commodities, [as if they were] not intelligent, and constantly dismissed other people's ideas. There was no balance. Today, I still stay in touch with the people that used to work for Tom. He changed all our lives by giving us new opportunities, but it's unfortunate and sad that when we reminisce, all we remember is how badly he treated everyone.

Joe's story shows that negative role models can be as influential as positive ones in shaping behaviors and leading to changes in our own identity. As a young professor, I had the good fortune of many positive role models. However, it was the behavior of one powerful negative role model that shaped my identity more than I understood at the time. She had reached the highest position in academia. By all accounts, she was successful. But much like Tom in Joe's story, she used her power to belittle and diminish those around her. Every time I witnessed her behavior toward others or experienced it myself, my thought was *I never want to be like her.*

Daniel, another of my former students, wrote that his early leadership experience taught him that "the most important and rewarding aspect about leadership is the impact that you have on others around you." Here's his story.

> I was a twenty-seven-year-old equity analyst at one of the largest firms in Colombia when I was given the opportunity of having a trial period as chief economist and strategist, leading a seven-member team.
>
> I understood why the company decided to set a trial period for me. I had some big shoes to fill, while becoming the youngest chief economist . . . and leading a team where several members were older than me. Having such a young face in this position could be a risk for the company in terms of customer confidence and trust.
>
> This understanding humbled me but also pushed me to work very hard on this challenge. I worked harder than anybody else in the company. After four years, I learned the importance of working hard, leading by example, overperforming, encouraging teamwork, and communications. However, the important and fulfilling experience for me was to see how the experience of the members in my team prepared [them] for a valuable career.
>
> Every single team member has evolved positively, and several of them have become protagonists in the Colombian financial market. I am so proud of them. For example, Nicolas has become the youngest director of financial planning and investor relations for the largest financial institution of Colombia.
>
> After his promotion he sent a note where he mentioned the following: "I believe that those first years of my professional life were an important foundation for my professional career and I appreciate all the guidance you provided during that time." Notes like these have made me realize that leadership is mainly about impacting others' lives and making them successful.

Activity 5.3 uses a simple two-step framework to link insight to action. Let's review the framework so you're able to apply it in any situation that requires problem solving.

STEP ONE: ANALYSIS. After you identify and describe the content for a given topic or question, process that data to find insights based on your understandings. These insights should lead you to a deeper exploration of why this topic or question is important to you.

STEP TWO: ACTION. Your analysis will inform your future behavior, so think concretely about how you might link your new insights to actions that could improve your future self. Even if the actions you consider are small, know that small, sustainable changes in your behavior can be enormously impactful.

Consider Professor Faber's words of wisdom in Ray Bradbury's dystopian novel, *Fahrenheit 451:* "Number one, as I said, quality of information. Number two: leisure to digest it. And number three: the right to carry out actions based on what we learn from the interaction of the first two."

Faber's quote sums up well what we're trying to do here. What data do you have, how are you going to process it, and how are you going to act on it? These are questions to ask yourself—and ask them often.

ACTIVITY 5.3 Analyzing Impact

Identify three people who have had a significant impact on you—consider both positive and negative role models. Briefly describe why their lives had such an impact on you. Finally, consider how to apply what you have learned from them about how to become a better champion.

1. Who: _____

Why: _____

What I have learned: _____

_____

_____

_____

_____

2. Who: _____

Why: _____

What I have learned: _____

_____

_____

_____

3. Who: _____

Why: _____

What I have learned: _____

_____

_____

_____

_____

Questions Are More Important Than Answers

Often, we expect someone who is leading to know the answers to our questions—and maybe even to know the answer to every question. Odds are they don't have those answers, of course. And neither do you. That can be frustrating because people, in general, don't like uncertainty and ambiguity—they want answers. When choosing leadership, you have to think about how much everyone affected by your vision of the future can tolerate uncertainty and ambiguity. As you think about this, consider these quotes:

> Managers discuss difficult decisions of personal and professional responsibility, that the most useful guidance involves asking questions, not giving answers.
> —Joseph Badaracco

> Computers are useless. They can only give you answers.
> —Pablo Picasso

Do not now seek the answers, which cannot be given
you because you would not be able to live them. And the point
is, to live everything. Live the questions now. Perhaps you will
then gradually, without noticing it, live along
some distant day into the answer.
—Rainer Maria Rilke

Good questions outrank easy answers.
—Paul A. Samuelson

It's better to debate a question without settling it than to settle
a question without debating it.
—Joseph Joubert

Questions are tools that generalize across contexts;
Answers are context-specific.
—Linda Ginzel

How Can I Help?

Randy Lewis, the former Walgreens executive who recommended the movie *Temple Grandin,* visited my classroom to discuss how Walgreens built a new distribution center designed to employ differently-abled people. He asked students, "Pretend you are the head of human resources at Walgreens; what questions would you ask me?" Most people asked questions that were fairly concrete, such as, "What would be the ramifications if one of the employees were to get hurt?

But Lewis said that when this situation actually unfolded, the most useful question one of the company's HR leaders asked was, "How can I help?" When someone comes to you with a great idea, he said, that's the best question you can ask—of others and yourself.

When you interview or talk to people, here's a great question to ask: "What's the best question to ask you right now?" Try imagining that someone else has asked that of you. **How would you answer?**

Three Questions

When it comes to questions, I take inspiration from Grant Hagiya, a bishop in the United Methodist Church, who told me a story about a sentinel that began:

> A sentinel was standing guard at night when he heard a noise in the darkness. He called out a question, "Who are you?" As the noise grew louder, he called out a second question, "What are you doing?" Finally, as the stranger approached, the sentinel asked, "Where are you going?"

These three questions are useful outside of this story. They are central to understanding when we should make a choice to lead. The answers are fundamental to understanding your identity, your behaviors, and your journey. Ask these questions of yourself now, and write down your answers.

1. Who are you?

_____

2. What are you doing?

_____

3. Where are you going?

_____

Return to the sentinel's questions periodically. When you do, be sure to record your answers here. Notice how your answers change over time—that's evidence that you've been learning and growing.

The Russian writer Leo Tolstoy asked similar questions in the story "The Three Questions," which begins:

> It once occurred to a certain king that if he always knew the right time to begin everything; if he knew who were the right people to listen to, and whom to avoid; and, above all, if he always knew what was the most important thing to do, he would never fail in anything he might undertake.

CHOOSING LEADERSHIP

> And this thought having occurred to him, he had it pro-
> claimed throughout his kingdom that he would give a great
> reward to anyone who would teach him what was the right
> time for every action, and who were the most necessary peo-
> ple, and how he might know what was the most important
> thing to do.

While these three questions are different from the Bishop's sentinel's, they're still fundamental questions for you to answer now and track over time.

1. What is the right time to begin anything? _____

_____

_____

_____

2. Who are the right people to listen to?_____

_____

_____

_____

3. What is the most important thing to do at any given time? _____

_____

_____

_____

These exercises are intended to inspire you to reflect and explore your own motivations. The questions get at themes running from your past, through the present, and toward your future self. In choosing leadership, it's important to understand, explore, and try to get at the core of who you are and why you're doing what you're doing.

"The job of the executive is to ask perceptive questions." These are the words of Ed Wrapp, who originally presented his observations of top managers in the 1967 article "Good Managers Don't Make Policy Decisions."

What perceptive questions can help you develop self-understanding? Who or what has led you to hold the values most important to you? What are your core values? You can think of other perceptive questions on your own, over time. These can help you process lessons from your own life, and the answers can help you in your leadership journey. And remember: You are the only person who can provide these answers.

At each decision point, you will need to ask, "What inspires me to make a risky choice to stand up for something, to change the future?" To prepare for that question, you have to develop self-knowledge, which will help you understand your journey. And when the time comes to make the risky choice, you'll be able to act knowing the answer to the question.

CHAPTER 6

Being Wiser, Younger

For group learning, use Leadership Module 6.A: Counting Fs
(30 Minutes)

L et's collect some data: Count the number of times the letter F appears in this block of text:

FINISHED FILES ARE THE RE-

SULT OF YEARS OF SCIENTIF-

IC STUDY COMBINED WITH THE

EXPERIENCE OF MANY YEARS

> **?** QUESTIONS
>
> How many Fs did you find? _____
>
> Now go back and count the Fs again. How many did you find this time? _____
>
> Do it again, one last time. How many Fs did you find the third time? _____
>
> *Answers on page 112*

Automatic Default Settings

Defaults are biases—as are shortcuts, heuristics, and habits. All of these words basically mean the same thing. In social psychology, bias is a neutral word that doesn't have a negative connotation but simply means "tendency toward." Earlier in the book, I introduced my term of *normal neurotics*. Most of us are normal neurotics, and on a daily basis, we go around trying to maintain or enhance our self-esteem, which leads to a variety of predictable biases. It's important for us to recognize these biases because while they usually serve us well, they can also lead us astray. To that end, it helps to know some of the basic cognitive biases identified by social psychologists.

One of the most fundamental and pervasive of them is called *availability*, and we discussed it in Chapter 3. It indicates that things that are more available or accessible in our minds are over weighted in our judgments. There are at least two important occasions when some data is more available in your mind or memory than others: beginnings and endings. This particular default is the reason that hellos and goodbyes are so important. First impressions matter because of what is called the *primacy effect*. When we meet someone for the first time, that initial contact forms the basis for our judgment about that person. Endings, on the other hand, are magnified by the *recency effect*. Things that happened recently are more available in our memory. Think about your most recent annual performance review at work. That conversation likely focused on the most recent three months, rather than the prior nine. This could be good if those three months are very relevant when it comes to your future performance. But if you did something amazing earlier in the year, that is less likely to be brought up unless you make a conscious effort to do so.

Another tendency we have is *overconfidence bias*. Because normal neurotics are smart, we are often right—but we therefore think we're right more often than we are. Yet another is *hindsight bias*, which holds that because we usually make good predictions, when we look back and see the outcome of an event, we say, "Oh, yeah, I knew that all along." These biases typically serve us well—after all, they help to maintain or enhance our self-esteem—but also can get in the way of our ability to learn the right lessons from experience.

When you're acting on defaults, you don't notice things; you simply act. In order to make a different choice, we need to stop and notice what's going on. Warren Bennis argued that it is important for an executive to be a "first-class noticer," a term he picked up from Chicago's own Saul Bellow and which Bennis used to highlight the important skill of observation. I love this term because noticing can help you turn off whatever bias might be in play and may result in you making a better decision. Inspired by it, I created a First-Class Noticer award to recognize students who demonstrate this skill in my classroom.

Becoming a first-class noticer will help you when choosing leadership. Think about a specific goal you have set for yourself. By keeping the goal in mind, it will better frame your search for relevant information. Becoming a better noticer will help you collect the data you need to make better choices—including the choice to lead and change the world. If you are interested in exploring this topic in more depth, I recommend Max Bazerman's excellent book *The Power of Noticing*.

> "" **My grandmother did not waste. There was nothing that came into her kitchen that she didn't find a use for. And I feel the same way about experience and words...you'd be surprised how much people waste what they know.** —NIKKI GIOVANNI

So how many Fs are there? If you found six, congratulations! You are correct.

Many people fail to find six Fs and instead see three, four, or five. If you are in this group, it indicates that you approached the task with the strategy of reading, not counting. If you found three Fs each time you did this, you are an excellent reader. When reading for comprehension, we fixate on about 70 percent of the text and skip the other 30 percent—the little words and connectors such as "if," "or," "but," and "of." We don't see or hear them because those little connecting words are unimportant for understanding the gist of the text.

Reading is your default, your go-to strategy. As I have discussed, usually these defaults, habits, and shortcuts serve us well. But this exercise demonstrates that sometimes defaults don't work and may even lead you astray. In this task, I asked you to count, not read. If you defaulted to reading—because that's what excellent readers do—that got in the way of your success on this particular task.

This exercise is illustrative. It highlights an awareness of our default settings. **When might you experiment with your behavior in order to make a different choice?**

Action Skills and Insight Skills

Knowing not only when but how to turn off these defaults is another skill that takes practice. Here's a framework that has helped thousands of my students over the last thirty years.

When I was hired at the University of Chicago in 1992, Harry Davis and Robin Hogarth handed me an article they'd written, "Rethinking Management Education: A View from Chicago." It described a framework they used in the classroom that helped students become self-sufficient learners and achieve higher levels of personal performance.

This is their basic idea: Students arrived in the classroom with *domain knowledge*, real-world knowledge—such as knowing industry standards or a company's specific operating procedures—a person acquires on the job. Faculty provided formal instruction to transmit *conceptual knowledge*, such as discipline-based theories. Those two different knowledge types meshed in the classroom, and graduates went on to use their combined knowledge to manage firms big and small.

We can agree that conceptual and domain knowledge are important, but Davis and Hogarth created a framework that highlighted the importance of *behavior*: namely, of *action skills*, the ability to turn knowledge into action, and *insight skills*, the ability to learn the right lessons from experience. They suggested that professors could furnish students with an understanding of and appreciation for those behaviors, and they believed this could be done in part by providing opportunities to acquire and practice those skills in the classroom.

Before meeting Harry and Robin, I hadn't thought about how I could focus on behaviors when teaching people to be wiser, younger—that is, to extract more value from their everyday experiences. After all, if we learn from our experiences by default, everyone who is old should be wise—and that is not the case. As Benjamin Franklin said, "Experience is a dear teacher." "Dear" in this case means expensive, and it is expensive precisely because we *don't* learn from it by default.

Here is a process, based on the scientific method, through which we can turn happenings, as Saul Alinsky, the father of community organizing, described them, into experiences:

1. **EXPERIMENT** by turning off a default and trying a different behavior.
2. **PRACTICE** by repeating the new behavior across time and place.
3 **GATHER** feedback and collect the data of your experience in writing.
4. **REFLECT** on the patterns and trends in your data and use this new understanding to inform your next experiment.

Lather, rinse, and repeat.

Collecting the Data of Your Experience

You are never going to be younger than you are today, but in order to be wiser, you will need to collect and record the data of your own experience. You don't necessarily learn automatically from your successes or failures. In order to digest a happening, you need data: you need to write it down. Writing forces you to prioritize what you think is important and worthy of saving for further analysis.

Repeat this aloud: "If you don't write it down, it doesn't exist."

When you record data across time, reviewing that data will help you see trends in your behavior. You can see whether the pattern of outcomes is improving, declining, or staying flat. When it comes to choosing leadership, this data can be just as valuable as the data from scholars in psychology, economics, and other disciplines. So be systematic about observing, collecting, and analyzing the data of your experience to determine if your experiments are successful. Examine the data and try again. It all starts with writing: If you don't record your results, they're essentially a figment of your imagination. Data needs to be seen, observable by yourself and others, so the data in your mind isn't actually data at all. When you write, you are creating something that didn't exist before and which can continue to be refined to benefit your future self.

It can help to put data you record into a framework. Earlier, you created a vicarious learning framework (Activity 4.1, page 71), the point of which was to help you structure data so you can learn from it. That framework was a draft, to be improved and further customized. Remember, it doesn't have to be perfect. Most any framework is better than none at all.

In the book *Winning Decisions*, authors J. Edward Russo and Paul J. H. Schoemaker present a four-step framework for making decisions: first, frame a decision, then gather intelligence, come to a conclusion, and learn from feedback. Russo and Schoemaker encourage you to collect enough data to keep track of the lessons of experience and to establish a system for learning from the results of past decisions. I love that their framework has the goal of developing your insight skills built into the fourth step of their decision-making process. Even if you have a little bit of structure to guide decision making, that's better than having nothing at all. And if that structure has the goal of learning from experience built in, even better!

 Ideas pass through most minds without taking in any substance or leaving any trace.
—A. R. AMMONS

Playing to Your Strengths

For group learning, use Leadership Module 6.B: Focus on Strengths (60 Minutes)

Here's the story of Henry, who told me that his first leadership experience taught him to highlight strengths of the organization rather than pinpoint its weaknesses:

> I had been working as an inside sales associate for Ferguson in Baltimore right out of college. An opportunity came up to lead our newest branch, located in Westfield, Massachusetts . . . with no wife and no kids, I jumped at the chance and relocated. My first leadership experience came when I arrived

at the new branch and had twelve associates (all older than myself). The organization structure wasn't nearly as efficient as my previous branch, and before leaving my boss had mentioned that processes needed to be cleaned up at this new branch. However, I didn't go in and start shaking things up off the bat. I worked in the shop at every station with every employee, understanding WHY they handled things the way they did. For about a month, I understood the reasoning behind previous decisions (how we got here) and, more importantly, the mindset of each individual I would lead (what is the engagement level). This allowed me to gain the trust of my employees and confidence to make decisions without insecurity of breaking up a valuable process. Despite some organizational challenges, the overall quality of the shop was second to none. I came to the Westfield branch with a goal of making it more like Baltimore . . . when promoted to another position back in Baltimore, I left Massachusetts with a goal of making Baltimore more like Westfield.

In *The Effective Executive*, Peter Drucker discusses how to make strengths productive and advises executives not to dwell on their weaknesses. Start with what you have, he says, not with what you don't have. You'll likely never be great at what you're weak at—and if you expend energy trying to be great at it, any gains you make will come at a cost. He devotes an entire chapter to "making strengths productive" and explains that playing to your strengths

is as much an attitude as it is a practice. But it can be improved with practice. If one disciplines oneself to ask about one's associates—subordinates as well as superiors—"What can this man do?" rather than "What can he not do?" one soon will acquire the attitude of looking for strength and of using strength. And eventually one will learn to ask this question of oneself.

Drucker calls it a "moral imperative" to focus on strengths, going on to say that "to focus on weakness is not only foolish; it is irresponsible." His words give me hope that executives will come to view leveraging strengths, more than overcoming weaknesses, as a development opportunity.

> **Wisdom is by far the chief element of happiness.**
> —SOPHOCLES

In the 2004 movie *Taxi*, Queen Latifah's character quips to Jimmy Fallon's character that "for someone with so many strengths, you sure know how to play to your weaknesses." There's so much truth in that one comic sentence. You have myriad strengths, yet how often do you lead with your best self? Do you even know the details of your strengths? How can we better heed the advice of Benjamin Franklin, who said, "Hide not your talents. They for use were made. What's a sundial in the shade?"

? Why not work to improve your productivity and success by doing more of what you do well every day?

Your Reflected Best Self

The next activity provides a process for collecting and understanding data about your strengths. The goal is to help you to better understand and leverage your individual talents and develop a plan to make your actions more effective. The basis for this activity is described in a *Harvard Business Review* article titled, "How to Play to Your Strengths." The authors—Laura Morgan Roberts, Gretchen Spreitzer, Jane Dutton, Robert Quinn, Emily

Heaphy, and Brianna Barker—present a feedback tool called the Reflected Best Self (RBS), which offers an experience distinct from performance reviews. The typical review focuses on your problem areas, or what are traditionally referred to as "development needs." The RBS instead focuses on your strengths and is designed to help you to tap into talents you may not be aware of and use them to improve your future outcomes. I love the idea that leveraging strengths could also be considered a development need.

With a traditional 360-feedback review, you collect data from everyone you interact with—clients, reports, peers, bosses—then look for trends and patterns. This feedback process highlights strengths and weaknesses, but for many people, the default with a 360 review is to offer feedback on weaknesses. And as Drucker says, leading with your weaknesses is a wasted opportunity.

 We do not learn from experience . . . we learn from reflecting on experience. —JOHN DEWEY

ACTIVITY 6.1 Strengths Data

For this activity, you need to collect, organize, and analyze data. Begin by soliciting comments from family, friends, colleagues, and teachers. Ask for specific examples of times your strengths generated important benefits. Next, organize the data and search for common themes, putting them in a framework to develop a clear picture of your abilities. This is what the authors Roberts et al. call your "self-portrait." I think of it as a mosaic of your strengths.

Finally, redesign the way you get things done in order to leverage your strengths. In other words, how can you do more of what you do well every day? Is there a way you could change your activities somewhat to take more advantage of your strengths? We often have opportunities to do more of what we do well, but seldom identify and act on these opportunities.

The questions that you should ask in collecting and understanding your strengths data include:

? **1.** Who should I ask for feedback?

_____

_____

_____

_____

? **2.** How do my family, friends, colleagues, and teachers see my strengths?

_____

_____

_____

_____

? **3.** What common theme emerges from the data they provided?

_____

_____

_____

_____

? **4.** How will I convert this feedback into action?

_____

_____

_____

_____

Use this space to take notes and begin drafting a framework.

Esperanza: The Color of Hope

> I haven't abandoned my red pen but I'm using the green pen
> that you gave me much more extensively.
> —Bob Reum, CEO of Amsted Industries (in memory)

For many years now, and for everyone who attends one of my classes, workshops, or keynote speeches, I give the gift of a green pen. This pen has become so symbolic of my teaching that some of my students have taken to calling the color "Ginzel Green." Symbols, of course, can be used to communicate gist. The green pen is a tool to help you collect that data, but it can also remind you to be your own coach. I suggest you collect the trend data of your experience across time in green ink.

In my negotiations class, students participate in a role-play simulation. For example, one person might play the role of a buyer negotiating a deal while the other plays the role of a seller. Before participating in each negotiation exercise, students prepare in advance by completing a framework I created for them.

TABLE 6.1: Preparation Worksheet

	SELF (e.g., buyer)	COUNTERPARTY (e.g., seller)
Prioritized Interests & Positions	#1 _____ #2 _____ #3 _____ #4 _____	#1 _____ #2 _____ #3 _____ #4 _____
BATNA (Best Alternative to a Negotiated Agreement)		
Reservation Price		
Target/ Aspiration		
What is your opening move? Initial strategy and contingency plans:		

For any given simulation, students bring their completed worksheets to class, along with their green pens. And every week, after participating in the exercise, they give themselves feedback in green ink. They write the things they recognize that they missed on their preparation worksheet and underscore what they correctly anticipated would happen. Notes to themselves can include skills and behaviors they want to practice in their next negotiation, as well as things that surprised them. Over the course of several simulations, they can see trends and patterns in the green ink. They become their own coach.

You don't need to be in a negotiations class to do this exercise. You are constantly faced with actual negotiations—not simulated ones—and whether in writing or not, you are always preparing for these real-life situations. You are diagnosing and analyzing situations in order to approach them in a more informed way. You can become your own coach, just like my students learn to do when they're filling out, analyzing, and learning from their preparation worksheets. You can collect the data of your experience—and just think how much wiser you will be at a younger age if you start doing this now.

How might you use the green pen in your life? Say you are anticipating an important meeting, tough problem, or difficult decision. Write out your advance preparation. In that worksheet, describe your goals, and explore the details of what you're trying to accomplish. Identify your bottom line, outline your approach, and consider your Best Alternative to a Negotiated Agreement (BATNA).

When it's time to go to the meeting or confront your challenge, take your written preparation as well as your green pen. Then, in green ink, write down the things that you didn't think about beforehand that ended up happening. If you can't do this during the discussion, then take the time to do it immediately after. Write notes to yourself in the margin of your own preparation worksheet. Underline things that happened as you predicted. Cross out whatever went differently than expected. The more green ink you see, the better. The Chilean poet Pablo Neruda said that he wrote in green ink because green is the color of *esperanza*—hope, in Spanish. Green is good!

When writing with your green pen, engage in participant-observation, a research method where the observer is a player in the action—simultaneously being in the moment (acting) as well as looking at trends and patterns in behavior (observing). The ability to be both in the action and to observe it at the same time is an important skill. We don't typically observe ourselves in a situation because we're so busy acting, but it's important to practice observing. Here are some questions that can help you practice being a participant-observer in a meeting or any other repeat situation.

1. What do you notice this time that is different from the last time?

2. How do you understand the current purpose?

3. Do you have questions that you didn't have last time?

4. What new ideas or associations come to mind?

Embrace the idea of being both in the action and observing it. For example, during a negotiation or any problem-solving situation, it takes practice to be your own coach. But with your preparation in hand, your green pen may help to serve as a reminder.

 The definition of insanity is doing the same thing over and over again and expecting different results. —ATTRIBUTED TO ALBERT EINSTEIN

Exit Ticket 3-2-1

For group learning, use Leadership Module 6.C: Exit Ticket
(10 Minutes)
Everything you've done in this chapter has reinforced the importance of noticing, asking for, collecting, and organizing data in an order that you can use to change your behavior. Here's another way to practice this.

To extract more value from the material in this chapter, try this framework for capturing data. It was provided by Todd Hellman, a former student, and can be applied to any experience. I have tweaked the framework slightly to reflect what you've been learning. Three simple questions provide a structure for deciding what data to collect and how to organize it.

ACTIVITY 6.2 Exit Ticket

What are **THREE** things you learned in Chapter 6?

1. _____

_____

_____

2. _____

_____

3. _____

_____

What are **TWO** things you are excited about and will share with others?

1. _____

_____

2. _____

_____

What is **ONE** question you still have, having finished this chapter?

1. _____

_____

_____

CHAPTER 7

Developing Leadership Skills Every Day

For group learning, use Leadership Module 7.A: Be Wiser, Younger (30 Minutes)

"He is a born leader." How many times have you heard that phrase, or a similar one about people being born with "it"? But as I've tried to show, this way of thinking is misguided. To understand why, imagine a normal distribution that represents the leadership capacity of everyone reading this book.

FIGURE 7.1: Average Leadership Capacity

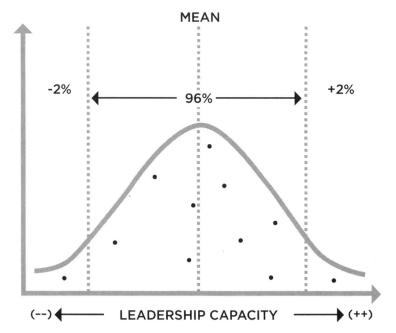

As shown in Figure 7.1, most of us—96 percent—are somewhere around the mean or average level of leadership capacity. The other 4 percent are outliers, either positive or negative.

I don't know if you are a negative outlier, and you probably don't know either. But if you are, I'm very sorry, because that means whatever "it" is, you were probably born without it.

Of course, you could be a positive outlier. Once again, you don't know if this describes you, but if it does, you have "it"! You had "it" when you picked up this book, and you're going to have "it" when you put it down. Nothing on these pages will harm or affect you negatively in any way. You are on a rocket ship to the moon.

This book is for the rest us, who exist somewhere between these two extremes. Wherever you are on this distribution, you have the opportunity to develop your courage, capacity, and wisdom. You can use data to create frameworks that will help you to accomplish your vision of the future. Your hard work in personalizing your learning will move you up that curve toward having more leadership capacity.

Figure 7.2: Be Wiser, Younger

As shown in Figure 7.2, some of us have farther to move, and some of us will move farther. But when people ask me, "Can you really teach all that leadership stuff? You're either born with it or not, right?" my answer is this: very few people are born with "it," and very few people aren't. But most of us can be wiser, younger; most of us can enhance our leadership capacity; and most of us can establish a new and higher mean level of capacity for ourselves.

This includes more than you—it includes almost everyone you encounter daily, be they family members, colleagues, or friends and neighbors. While you are developing your own leadership skills, you can also be developing the leadership capacity of people around you. This is a lesson from social psychology, and it's a lesson you can put to work at home, on the job, and in your community. You can create strong environments that move yourself and other people in a more productive direction.

As Kurt Lewin said, "there's nothing so practical as a good theory." Theories are practical because they help you create frameworks, and frameworks allow you to organize your data in efficient, effective ways, so that you can extract your own lessons from that data when you need it to inform your actions. You may not have had particular theories in mind when creating frameworks in this book, but social psychological theories have underpinned most everything you've written.

This book represents a meta-framework for organizing the data of your experience, and its pages collectively represent a strong environment that can help you craft your own perspective on leadership. Given the limited number of pages in this book, I have focused on behavioral choices that can help you create a better future for yourself—tomorrow, next month, or next year.

From this point forward, you will make choices, and only you will know whether those choices have helped you accomplish your goals.

> I'm more passionate about maximizing each individual's potential and measuring how they are growing than trying to unlock the keys to business leadership insight. If we focus in on each person's individual growth everyone wins and at the individual level it is all encompassing not just business success. —MARK AGNEW, PRESIDENT AND CEO OF LOU MALNATI'S PIZZERIA

Busting Leadership Myths

For group learning, use Leadership Module 7.B: Leadership Myth Busting (25 Minutes)

Most people believe that behavior is a function of personality. You may hear statements such as "You are the way you are because you are an ENTJ," which refers to a personality type on the Myers-Briggs type indicator, where the initials stand for Extraversion, Intuition, Thinking, Judgment. You may hear, "You are a high sensation seeker," or "You are a firstborn"—or "You're a cucumber," or a "pickle," or whatever the personality-category label. Labels such as these put causality into trait words and have the effect of placing the cause of behavior squarely inside of you.

But Lewin's equation, which we covered back in Chapter 2, upends the notion that leadership is about personality traits. Someone who is aggressive in one situation might not be inherently aggressive and could be gentle and kind in a different situation. You can't change characteristics that are inside of you, but it is possible to change your behavioral choices.

There are a lot of other myths about who leaders are and what they look like. Myths are unproven, oversimplified beliefs that may not accurately reflect reality, but that we unquestioningly accept as true. What myths have you heard about leadership—or chosen to believe—that might not be true? Here's the beginning of a list, and you can add to it:

1. Leaders are born good leaders.

2. Leaders have charisma.

3. Leaders are extroverts.

4. Leaders don't make mistakes.

5. You can't lead if you aren't the leader.

6. Leadership is based on seniority.

7. Leaders have all the answers.

8. You can clearly spot a leader.

9. Leaders need followers.

10. _____

11. _____

12. _____

13. _____

14. _____

15. _____

16. _____

17. _____

18. _____

19. _____

20. _____

Here, in Jennifer's story, she writes about how she was able to recognize and reject leadership mythology based on gender:

Leadership started at a later age for me than most. As the only child of immigrant parents, the focus was the path that my parents had laid out for me with the best of intentions. I did not have much decision-making power, nor did I demand it. However, life evolved and so did I. Having spent my entire career in finance, my earliest encounters with leadership were distinct. Leadership was male, fierce, and potent. Leaders at the trading firm I worked for inspired greatness and fear. So, when my first leadership opportunity came about, I emulated the same false bravado that most of the trading floor exhibited. The two young trading assistants were capable but required different motivation factors and leadership styles that I had trouble recognizing at the time. My expectation was that I would lead, lay out a plan, and they would follow. This worked really well for Sheila. For the second trading assistant, this worked poorly. She resented being micromanaged and often disregarded the hierarchy, asking my manager for things like vacation and [to weigh in on] differences of opinion. She eventually left the firm, and team conflict was likely a factor. Having invested so much in her development and training, I resented her for leaving yet failed to see my part in the situation.

Fast forward twelve years, I find myself the leader of mixed-gender teams of varying backgrounds and ages. I generally lead a junior team of three to four members and am responsible for complex analysis and client presentations that are then delivered to the C-Suite of companies big and small. The individuals I lead are usually eager to perform well and have exceptional academic backgrounds. Although I am still in finance, leadership looks and feels very different today.

Leadership can be female, and it can be soft as well as tough. I finally found a voice and my leadership toolkit is a lot more complex than fear and motivation; it includes reading people and situations in order to apply the right calibration of motivation, purpose, responsibility, and consequences. Today, leaders rule by reason, not by absolute authority, and my definition of a leader is someone who inspires confidence, is capable, and can react to and successfully navigate ambiguity. A leader does not have to have all the answers; however, a leader should be able to arrive at them.

The leader I am today has evolved as a function of self-awareness and development but also as a result of the shift in societal norms, with women representing not only a greater percentage of the workforce but also a greater percentage of leadership positions. I look forward to reflecting upon the leader I will be in the next decade.

Jennifer's story asks us to consider what kind of benefits there are in believing such myths and what kind of price we pay in believing them. She describes how she grew to articulate her own thinking about how leadership looks and feels. It is hard to reject leadership mythology because it is so deeply ingrained in our culture. But the fact is this: Leadership is a behavior, and factors like gender and personality type have very little to do with it.

As I wrote earlier, Duke's Rick Larrick has challenged people to talk about leadership as a behavior as opposed to a person or a position. It's time for you to take up this challenge and make it your reality. In everyday conversation, stop using the nouns "leader" and "manager." Use verbs instead: "to lead" and "to manage."

A person can have the title of CEO but not engage in leadership behaviors. And even if a person has the title and engages in leadership behaviors, that person cannot possibly lead all of the time. Leadership is independent of title, just as it is independent of a particular list of personality traits or other such attributes, including your own list of competencies. We have management and leadership, not managers and leaders. You are a champion who decides when to manage and when to lead.

> **We define ourselves by the choices we have made. We are, in fact, the sum total of our choices.** —PROFESSOR LOUIS LEVY (MARTIN BERGMANN) IN THE MOVIE *CRIMES AND MISDEMEANORS*

Think Like a Social Psychologist

Adopt social psychological explanations for behavior, rather than more personality-based approaches. When you think like a social psychologist, you will think more complexly about situations and context.

In general, people tend to act as though 80 to 90 percent of what causes an action is inside of a person. But in what social psychologists call "strong situations," it's the reverse—80 to 90 percent of behavior could be due to something outside of the person.

Take a classroom as an example of a strong situation. If you were in my leadership course, sitting among other executives, you would look around and see an enormously diverse group of people. Yet although each person would be different, each would be behaving in the same way. Most would be taking notes. If I were to attempt a joke, most people would attempt to laugh. This is generally accepted classroom behavior. The classroom environment is designed to encourage classroom behavior. Consider the physical layout of the room, which in my case is auditorium seating around a central pit. You have to turn your body away from the front of the room in order not to look directly at the professor.

A strong situation affects behavior, and you affect the situation. Don't underestimate the role you play in creating your environment. Instead, use the power of the situation to your advantage.

This will take some getting used to. Although there is a connection between what you do and what you get, we often look at other people and think that their behavior is due to issues involving *them* and little else. In doing so you fail to realize that you are a big part of their situation, and thus their behavior. Don't go through your days discounting the impact that your actions have in eliciting behavior from those around you.

Just like a professor in a classroom, you can create situations that move people's behavior in more productive directions. That's the gist of social psychology: to change someone's behavior, change their situation—not the person.

To gain a better handle on the link between what you do and what you get, experiment with your behavior. Try being nice when you wouldn't ordinarily, for example. You'll probably find that the kindness comes back at you because reciprocity is a powerful force in behavior. There are two kinds of reciprocity: positive and negative. If I am kind, warm, and charitable to my coworker, she will generally reciprocate in kind. If I am cold, condescending, and belittling, she will reciprocate that, too.

Armed with this understanding of the fundamentals of social psychology, you have a responsibility to use your wisdom to build strong situations.

To learn more about how to think like a social psychologist, I recommend that you read Nicholas Epley's book *Mindwise*.

Stay in the Question

For group learning, use Leadership Module 7.C: The Zeigarnik Effect (20 Minutes)

Reject leadership myths. Create strong environments. Here's a third thing you can do: stay in the question. Champions have a bias for action, but it is also important to practice "staying in the question," or accepting instances where you don't have closure. Not having an answer to a question can feel uncomfortable, but the ability to stay in the question is a skill, and the courage to practice this skill will serve your future self.

Bluma Zeigarnik, an early psychologist, is known for having discovered what is now called the *Zeigarnik effect*—the tendency to remember uncompleted or interrupted tasks better than completed ones.

According to Maria Konnikova, writing on the *Scientific American* blog *Literally Psyched*, in 1927 Zeigarnik

> . . . noticed a funny thing: waiters in a Vienna restaurant could only remember orders that were in progress. As soon as the order was sent out and complete, they seemed to wipe it from memory. Zeigarnik then did what any good psychologist would: she went back to the lab and designed a study. A group of adults and children was given anywhere between 18 and 22 tasks to perform (both physical ones, such as making clay figures, and mental ones, such as solving puzzles)—only, half of those tasks were interrupted so that they couldn't be completed. At the end, the subjects remembered the interrupted tasks far better than the completed ones—over two times better, in fact.

The Zeigarnik effect results from the psychological tension inherent in an unfinished task, a tension that arises from ambiguity and the lack of closure that comes with task completion. You experience Zeigarnik anytime an answer suddenly comes to you when you're not necessarily working on that problem or even thinking about it. You wake up in the morning with a solution to something that has been bothering you. Or an idea comes to you while you're in the shower. Once you "put a ribbon on it" and mentally put it away, you stop thinking about it. It is gone from your mind. We tend to like to tie things up neatly, to seek closure and move on. But being comfortable with ambiguity is a skill that benefits from practice.

It is said that Ernest Hemingway had a method for harnessing the energy of the Zeigarnik effect. When he finished working at the end of the day, he stopped writing midsentence and picked up there at the start of the next day. The tension from the unfinished task increased the probability that his transition was productive from day to day.

This same idea has been expressed by others, including the late Jonathan Z. Smith from the University of Chicago Divinity School, who said, "I always try, but I don't always succeed, to leave my class on an incomplete sentence."

Executives can also benefit from harnessing the Zeigarnik effect. Remember that the ability to handle ambiguity is among the most-sought-after executive skills. My hope is that you will practice staying in the question, where creativity energy and anxiety often reside together. Begin feeling comfortable being uncomfortable, rather than rushing to closure. Do the hard work of increasing your capacity to deal with uncertainty. May Zeigarnik be with you.

We take reflection to be that space suspended between experience and explanation, where the mind makes the connections.
—JONATHAN GOSLING AND HENRY MINTZBERG

Develop Your Own Point of View

Like it or not, you will need to embrace the Zeigarnik effect when you finish this book. That's because this last chapter isn't really an ending; it's more the beginning of your independent leadership journey.

As a student of leadership, you are tasked with developing your own point of view. Your perspective will evolve with experience and understanding of your own identity. You determine what matters most to you in choosing leadership. In *On Becoming a Leader*, Bennis wrote, "Perspective is no more and no less than how you see things, your particular frame of reference. Without it, you're flying blind. But it is also your point of view."

Bill George, a Harvard Business School professor and former CEO of Medtronic, wrote in *Harvard Business Review*, "During the past fifty years, leadership scholars have conducted more than one thousand studies in an attempt to determine the definitive styles and characteristics and general personality traits of great leaders. None of these studies have produced a clear profile of the ideal leader."

And here's Bob Sutton, writing on his blog *Work Matters:* "Tens of thousands of books have been written on leadership and there are several academic journals dedicated entirely to this subject. . . . So the task of reviewing leadership literature—and acting on it as a leader—isn't to understand it all (that is impossible), but to develop a point of view on the few themes that matter most."

ACTIVITY 7.1 Point of View

What is your point of view on the leadership themes covered in this book? Figure out what themes matter most to you and record them here.

You can be more proactive in your own journey by referring back to what you have written here as a way to help you figure out what matters most to you. As you wrestle with that, you'll determine the enduring values, aspirations, and guiding principles driving your choices. When you reveal those to yourself, you will be able to make better choices and bring more meaning to your life. The cumulative impact of your everyday choices can make a huge difference at work, in your family, community, and society.

Create Your Own Activities

You are free to experiment with behavior and create different frameworks that will help build your capacity and wisdom. Every day you observe, collect data, and decide how best to organize and process it. So now it is your turn to identify sources—Ted Talks, speeches, books, movies, or other summary materials—to use as the basis for creating your own leadership development activities.

Many years ago, the amazing educator Miriam Kass, who is now the Principal of Akiba-Schechter Jewish Day School in Chicago (and who credits *The Art of Teaching Reading* by Lucy Calkins) gave me a general framework that I have applied to developing leadership at the movies. Choose a film to watch and consider three types of connections:

1. **Text-to-film connections**—integrating specific concepts presented in readings with something seen in a film.
2. **Self-to-text/film connections**—integrating your own life experiences with something either read or seen in a film. These connections can include events in your past or those that you anticipate in the future.
3. **Text-to-text connections**—integrating concepts from one reading with those from another reading.

Making these connections will help you process and customize your understanding of these sources. Kass's framework offers a simple way to draw personalized lessons from a source and make it relevant for you. The purpose of the activity is to form meaningful connections between everyday materials and experiences in order to reach original insights. Your reflections and insights will shape your thinking and behavior.

Keep these connections in mind as you come across sources and summaries. If you watch a film, you won't have an accompanying required reading. Instead, you'll need to come up with perceptive questions to ask yourself: what is in your past, or learning repertoire, that you can use to inspire questions and deeper reflection?

On your leadership journey, and on your own, you need to turn happenings into experiences. You will do that by integrating your self-knowledge with what's outside of you. Don't simply accept the director's take, or the critics', or the professor's, or mine. The way I make connections is different from the way you do. Understand what that film means to *you*. What's the gist? Leadership can be taught, but only up to a point. There's only so much you can learn in a classroom or from a book. Ultimately, you have to take lessons and make them your own. You took a big first step when you made the choice to develop your leadership skills. But this is the journey of a lifetime, and it's a journey that can take a lifetime.

> " In the end, you know, we are very minor blips in a cosmic story. Aspirations for importance or significance are the illusions of the ignorant. All our hopes are minor, except to us; but some things matter because we choose to make them matter. What might make a difference to us, I think, is whether in our tiny roles, in our brief time, we inhabit life gently and add more beauty than ugliness. —JAMES MARCH

ACTIVITY 7.2 Final Paper

Writing assignments provide you with an opportunity to consider the personal impact and relevance of the source you've chosen. Keep that in mind as you consider writing your final paper. This is the most substantial activity in this book. I included it for you because former students have told me that this writing assignment changed their life. It has the opportunity to change your life, too.

This is an homage to my oft-mentioned Booth colleague and friend Harry Davis, who makes this assignment at the end of his long-standing Business Policy course: a ten-page paper about your professional and/or personal strategy.

1. **Subject:** Focus primarily on you and explore important strategy questions in the context of your professional and/or personal life. You should include some relevant history, assess the current situation, and develop some strategic thinking or plans as you look forward.

2. **Timeframe:** Select a timeframe appropriate to the questions you have raised. This could be as short as next year or as long as the next twenty or thirty years.

3. **Links to the book:** Frame your paper in a manner you find useful. Consider using one or more of the concepts from this book because they may provide a useful structure or perspective. Remember, however, that the purpose of including such concepts is not to provide a formal summary or review of course material.

4. **Hints:** Think about the question, "What could I write about that I will find valuable to reread in three, ten, or even twenty years?" Some former students have kept a journal during the class as a way of generating some raw material for the paper.

Try hard to write this paper for *you*. Harry has suggested that students should revisit their paper every few years to update their personal and professional strategies. Use the lined pages provided at the end of this book to begin recording your ideas.

Taking Your Next Steps

You have an opportunity to make a bigger difference in your life than you are making right now. It is my hope that this book will help you in choosing leadership. While I wrote that this is the end of this book, I must amend that: I hope it will actually continue to serve you in the years ahead, holding as it does your evolving definitions, customized frameworks, and personal reflections. Take Activity 7.3 below as an example. Writing your current definition of leadership is a great way to make progress since your first-draft definition in Activity 2.4. Then, in the next month, six months, two years from now—whenever is the next time you pick up this book and look through your own words on its pages—reconsider your definition. How did it change? How did *you* change? Your life is a work in progress, and this book is your companion. It is a container for storing notes important to your everyday leadership development. And it is an invitation to continue collecting and organizing the data of your experience. The source of your own individualized wisdom is in your hands.

We opened with John F. Kennedy's quote, "Leadership and learning are indispensable to each other." While Kennedy never had the opportunity to deliver these words—they were written as part of the speech he planned to give on the day of his assassination—we have the opportunity to *live* them by making learning indispensable to leadership in our lives.

ACTIVITY 7.3 Current Definition of Leadership

Draft a definition of leadership that reflects the world of possibilities. Don't let your default definition create self-imposed limits.

_____

_____

_____

_____

PART 2

Leadership Modules

Introduction Leadership Modules

Leadership Modules are provided for activities in each chapter to facilitate group learning from the workbook.

LEADERSHIP MODULE A: Building Community
(40 Minutes)

This is not a typical class. It's a class *all about you*.

It really is.

I created the concept of Leadership Capital because I saw that the interest in leadership development had fueled a giant industry that was (and still is) a mess. In this industry, people will sell you anything leadership-related that you're willing to buy. But despite all the books, manuals, personality tests, and more, it remains true that we don't know what leadership is.

That's because the definition changes depending on the person. It hinges on *you*. In this course, one of the things I'm going to do is help each student to figure out their own definition of leadership. That means you will be creating your own definition.

To start this process, we are going to spend a few minutes introducing ourselves to the class, and I know that when some people hear this, they think, "What a waste of time!" They'd rather check their email or do something else. But the time spent on introductions has us practicing two important skills: active listening and community building.

Look around the room, and quickly calculate how long each one of us can speak in the time we have together. Because you'll only be "on" briefly during the introductions, you're going to have extra cognitive capacity most of the time, and you can use it in one of two ways: You can check out by checking your email, daydreaming, or doodling, or you can practice skills. Skills are behaviors that benefit from practice, and right now you have the opportunity to practice active listening and community building.

One of the things executives have often said to me is, "You've got to teach my employees how to listen." Most people hear, but they don't listen, which is why it is important to learn active listening. We can practice this when doing other things, like introductions.

Right now, practice being in the present and staying in the moment. You may start thinking about all the other important things that you have to do, but actually, you don't know that they are any more pressing than what we're about to do. You don't yet know how important it is for you to be listening in this moment, while you're here with me. You have a chance to make the most of our time together, but you might sacrifice some of what we're learning in order to think about other things, which would effectively make this experience more expensive for you.

Benjamin Franklin is often misquoted as having said, "Experience is the best teacher." The real quote is "Experience is a dear teacher"—"dear" as in expensive. Experience is an expensive teacher because we so rarely learn from it. When you succeed at something, you often think, "Yes! *I* did that! I'm smart and good, and that's the reason for my success." Meanwhile when you fail at something, you might attribute the failure to something else, like bad luck. You're either praising yourself or protecting yourself, and either way you're learning nothing from your experiences— or learning the wrong lessons.

Here's what we're going to do: Tell us your name, what your nine-year-old self wanted to do when you grew up, and the first word that comes to your mind when you hear the word "leader." This exercise is going to move quickly, and I'd like you to try listening closely to what people say and how they say it. Do they use humor? What words do they mention, and how? Do you have anything in common with them? Do they say something that makes you want to connect with them, or to learn something more about them? Stay engaged. Stay present. That's a big part of active listening.

We are a community. We are going to learn together during this course, and one of the ways you learn is by experimenting with your own behaviors. You have to take risks to learn, and once you leave this classroom, it will get harder to take these risks. This is our chance to build community so that we will feel more comfortable learning together.

LEADERSHIP MODULE B: Beginnings and Endings (15 Minutes)

Please humor me. I want to ask you all to get out your cellphones and take a selfie. I'm going to do it, too. I want to draw your attention to beginnings and endings, and this selfie will help. It records where you are right now, at the beginning of our journey.

This class is rooted in the academic discipline of social psychology, which is about understanding individual behavior in a social context. Executives need to know social psychology because they need to be able to put interpersonal dynamics into an actionable context. In this class, I am going to teach each of you how to think more like a social psychologist. I want you to leave here with the ability to take an idea and turn it into an action. If you have a concept in mind, you need to be able to transform it into a behavior in order to improve your future outcomes.

Let's start with a finding from social psychology called the *availability bias.* Bias is not a bad word in psychology, it simply means a "tendency toward." We all systematically process things in a biased way, and the things that are available in your mind are overrepresented in your judgments and your decisions. Things that are salient, come to mind, and capture your attention are over weighted in your judgments. This is the *availability bias,* and it's a reliable tendency. I call these kinds of tendencies "defaults," like a default setting on your computer that runs automatically in the background unless you change it.

Be mindful of beginnings and endings, such as how you begin a meeting, end a project, or start and end a course. When you meet someone or start a program, the first things that happen sets the tone. This is why first impressions are so powerful.

Endings are important, too, because things that happened recently are more accessible in your memory. That is the *recency bias.*

Every new year, people make resolutions and state what they want to do or change in the upcoming year. If you want to achieve your goals, you have to figure out how to make your intentions salient so that you're more likely to turn an intention into an action.

Our next activity is along these lines. I want you to pick one word to keep available in your mind. Find a sticky note and a pen. (I prefer green.) Please use the pen to write on the note a single word that summarizes what you want to focus on during this class. I'll give you a few minutes to think about what you want to write. When you're finished, stick it somewhere you will see it during class.

By putting your note on, say, the cover of your book, the word you wrote will stay salient. Former Chicago Booth professor Robin Hogarth has suggested using whatever goal or idea that you want to keep salient as your email password so that you will be reminded of it every time you log in.

Social psychology teaches us more about how to keep our goals and ideas salient, as well as about how to make ideas salient for others. The sticky note provides one way you can put this idea into action, but there are many others. All it takes is a little time and structure, so . . . . what do you want to make salient?

LEADERSHIP MODULE C: Choosing Leadership
Introduction (10 Minutes)

Video: Introduction to *Choosing Leadership*
https://www.choosingleadershipbook.com/

Video transcript:

Hi, I'm Linda Ginzel, and we're here at the University of Chicago.

I teach here, at Booth, at the business school. I actually teach leadership to our Executive MBA students in Hong Kong, London, and Chicago, and as a result of my teaching, I created a book.

Now, you would think a business school professor who teaches executives and writes a book about leadership... that the book would be for executives.

But actually, this book is for you. This workbook is intended to help people everywhere—preschool teachers, coaches, executives—to develop their courage, their capacity, their wisdom, so that everyone can be wiser, younger. And the workbook is a compilation of a variety of exercises and activities . . . ideas that I've developed over the course of over thirty years teaching here at the

University of Chicago.

And at one point, people said to me, "Can I get an extra copy of this for my boss?" or "My wife would love this book, is there a way I could get another copy?"

And I would say, "No, only one copy per student. Because it's a handout for my class."

And I thought, Why . . . why should it be that only the students who come to the University of Chicago, the Booth School of Business, can develop their leadership skills by doing these activities and these exercises?

And that's how Choosing Leadership *was born organically, out of necessity. There are twenty activities that are specifically designed to help you to collect the data of your own experience. To help you to process lessons, to figure out what's important to you, when you step up to make a risky choice to change the future. What's your definition of leadership? Who's influenced you? And why?*

And then it teaches you how to create your own exercises . . . how to learn from everyday life, how to learn from movies, from TED Talks, from speeches. No matter what experience you have, if you process the lessons of those experiences, the idea is that you can be wiser, younger.

Then you get together with friends. You get together with family members, you get together with people you work with—and you teach and learn with each other.

It's great if you come to a place like the University of Chicago and take classes from professors. It's great if you go to talks and have experts come and tell you about leadership, for example. But just think how much wiser you can be at a younger age . . . if you also take more responsibility for your own growth, and for your own development.

This book—the workbook—is a way to help you to develop your ability to make better choices, to change the future. And that's when we champion a vision for a better tomorrow. Pick up a copy of Choosing Leadership, *grab some friends, and enjoy the leadership journey.*

You have this book, and please write your name at the front of it for two reasons. First, if you lose yours, there's a better chance that you'll get it back. But second, this is not a book that you read, absorb, and then put on the shelf. This is a book that you *do*. It's a container that's intended to hold your evolving self. That may sound strange, but I have already said that this course is all about *you*. This book is paperback, the size of a composition notebook, and meant to meet you where you are—whatever your stage of growth, reflection, or self-understanding.

This is about continuing your lifelong learning journey and setting you up to be your own coach so that you can be wiser, younger and so that you can explore important questions for yourself, with yourself, and with others—without a teacher guiding you. When you're ready to move forward or go deeper, the book will be there for you.

Chapter 1 Leadership Modules

LEADERSHIP MODULE 1.A: Early Leadership Story
(45 Minutes)

This image is called a reversible figure, and many of you have likely seen some version of this. There's another popular reversible figure that looks like an old lady and a young lady. And there's another that looks like both a duck and a rabbit.

Typically, we see black words on a white page. Anything figural is black, and the background is white. But in this case, someone made the figure white and the background black, which is why the image is unstable and you see the vase if you focus on the white or two faces in profile if you focus on the black. The word I want to convey by showing you this is *choice*. You're making a choice about what to see.

We have many more choices than we recognize, and leadership is one of them. We're going to open the next activity with a question: When do you choose to lead? I'm not asking why you lead, or how, or what you are trying to accomplish—but when. When do you stand up and make a choice to lead?

Video: Earliest Leadership Experience
https://www.youtube.com/watch?v=lS7LD0Ekym0

Video transcript:
Talking about leadership and questions that we might ask of ourselves and others about what it means to lead, a lot of questions might be, "well, how do you lead, or why do you lead? What do you do when you lead?" I think the most perceptive question is: when do you lead? If you think about leadership as a choice, a behavior that we take, that we choose, to create a different future, a better future, then I think it's a really interesting question to ask: When do you choose to lead? And in answering this question, it might help to get some data. The data is your earliest leadership experience. What do you choose? What did you choose or do you think about when you think about the one of the first times you exhibited leadership behavior?

Whatever that story is, it's important grist for the mill. It's important to help you understand when you stand up and make a risky choice to change the future. Over the years, I've asked this question to my students many times. And when I first started asking this question, I got what I thought was a very strange response. Very accomplished young adults would say to me, "Oh, I haven't had an opportunity to lead yet, so I don't have an earliest leadership experience," or "I'm just a manager, I haven't had an opportunity to lead. Someday! Someday I'll be a leader and then I'll be able to lead." And I realized, really, that we're inhibiting our own choices with whatever is our definition of leadership. But a lot of times we haven't understood our definition of leadership. So the question, "When do you choose to lead?" will help to unearth the assumptions, the substratum that you're using when you think about leadership.

All right, I'll tell you my earliest leadership story. I was in ninth grade and I was the president of my student council, and in my ninth grade year book, you'll see it says, "Student council has a very good year." And we did, we had a very good year. And the reason we had a very good year is because of volunteer council. Now, have you, do any of you in your junior high or high school, did you have volunteer council? I actually haven't ever had a yes to that question, because I created it. I did. Me, Linda Ginzel, ninth grade student council. I created the volunteer council, and the reason that student council had a very good year is because of the energy, efforts, dedication, the heart, the time and talent that the students of volunteer council put into our school. These are people who, for whatever reason, didn't run for student council, or maybe they ran and they didn't win. I don't know why they didn't have a seat at the table, so we created a seat at the table, and created volunteer council. It gave them a vehicle to put their energy into making the school a better place. They're the ones who were on the decoration committee. They're the ones who were on the clean-up committee. They're the ones who brought in speakers and had ideas. And so that's how I made a small choice to change the future at my junior high school. That's my earliest leadership experience. What does your earliest leadership experience say about when you choose to lead?

Now it's your turn. I want you to recall and describe one of your earliest leadership experiences. You'll have three minutes to write about it, then seven minutes to share what you wrote with your partner.

There's something in my story that speaks to what *I* associate with leadership. There's something in your choice that's going to be revealing about *your* definition. Whatever story you choose, recognize that there's a reason you're choosing it. Make your choice, write it in this book, then discuss it with your neighbor. The two of you will work together to figure out the underlying theme of your choice.

One student who took a *Leadership Capital* class was a rocket scientist from Argonne Labs. When we did this exercise, he recalled that when he was in kindergarten, a new student joined his class. While other kids weren't being mean to this new student, they weren't being particularly nice to him either. Our future rocket scientist saw that the new kid was being excluded so he went up to him during recess and brought him into a play group.

This was this scientist's earliest leadership experience, and there was obviously no official title involved. The interaction was peer-to-peer. But this story revealed to him that he valued bringing people together. Every person's story is different—whether it involves direct reports and bosses, hierarchy, parents and family, school and teachers, or titles and peers. You can turn to the Index and see a list of eleven leadership stories told in the book.

Ivan's story, 1
Connie's story, 17, 59
Daniel's story, 102
Henry's story, 115
Jake's story, 35
Jennifer's story, 130
Joe's story, 100
Laura's story, 48
Lena's story, 40
Sel's story, 18
Shilpa's story, 21

One thing I like to say is "if you don't write it down, it doesn't exist." If you don't have the data or any written record of your reflections, you won't remember them later. But if you do have data, you can turn to that data later and it could prove to be informative.

Take three minutes for quiet, individual reflection, as we need to reflect in order to learn and process life lessons. After that, take seven minutes to talk with your partner so that you can learn together. What is your earliest leadership experience? What was important about the choice you made to lead? What does your choice say about your definition of leadership? There are no right or wrong answers. Everyone selects a story based on what they believe leadership to be.

LEADERSHIP MODULE 1.B: Labels (30 Minutes)

Video: How Labels Manage Meaning

https://www.youtube.com/watch?v=hXgGM5BtxyI

Video transcript:

I've been on this mission to change the conversation around leadership. And part of that mission involves trying to use the words "managing" and "leading" as verbs, as opposed to "manager" and "leader" as nouns. This is hard. It's a lot harder to find a substitute for the word leader, particularly. The labels that we use manage meaning, and what we call ourselves and others really matters. In my classroom, when I teach executives, I try to use the word "executive." So, you're an executive and mostly you manage, and sometimes you lead. In the book, I use the word "champion." And the reason is that executive is more expansive than leader or manager, but champion is even more inclusive because a lot of people have their own stereotypes about what executive means. And they say, "Well, I'm not an executive," even if I try to use Drucker's definition, even if I tried to define it.

The use of "champion" actually came about as a result of a friend and colleague, Richard Thaler, suggesting that if I wanted this book to have a broad audience beyond my classroom, I needed to lose the word executive. And I'm grateful to him every day that he challenged me to come up with a label that would be more inclusive. And that's how I went from manager, leader, and executive to champion.

Now, the reason that labels are important. The reason that the words we choose to describe ourselves and others are so important is because it really reflects on our identity and becomes the basis for our behaviors. Labels are a way to manage meaning. They frame how you think about yourself and others.

Are any of you middle children? In your opinion, is there a positive or negative connotation around being a middle child? For some people, being a middle child is a positive part of their identity, and for others it's not. But, if for you, being a middle child is not positive, then that middle-child label can affect you negatively.

I once worked with a very capable, terrific young man who had a very strong identity as a middle child. And it was a negative identity for him. Every time something would go wrong, he would say, "Well, it's because I'm a middle child." I thought it was a very interesting, attributional kind of an explanation. Bad things were always associated with him being a middle child.

Then, I had a middle child of my own, and when he was younger, I don't know, three, four years old or something, we were in Israel. And he said to me, "Mom, why did that guy call me a sandwich child?" And I said, "Oh, you know, well, sandwich child, that's the translation from Hebrew for middle child." And I continued, "I'll tell you why. You're the only one in our family who has an older brother and a younger brother. It's like a sandwich. They're the bread, and you're the meat. You're the center of the sandwich." To this day, that boy has taken this as part of his identity. Really, if you say to him, "Oh, you're the middle kid." He'll say, "Oh, no, I'm the center of my family." And his email address to this day is thecenter@. It's so interesting, the labels we choose, to the labels we use to define ourselves and others. They matter because they manage meaning. So, think about whether your labels are inhibiting choices or enabling them. The words you choose are really important.

Labels apply in a big way to leadership. Instead of using the words "leader" and "manager" as nouns and labels, try to start using verbs, "to lead" and "to manage." The goal is to help you think more broadly about leading and managing as behaviors as opposed to people, roles, or positions. There are stereotypes around what it means to be a "leader" and what it means to be a "manager," but *Choosing Leadership* can enable people to make better choices instead of constraining themselves and others through stereotypes.

If we stop using the words "leader" and "manager," we need a noun that we can use as a substitute. What word should we use? Peter Drucker uses "executive," which is a practical and concrete option.

The words that we choose to use manage meaning, and I have found that it isn't helpful to think about some people as leaders and other people as managers. It's more helpful to think about people who sometimes manage and sometimes lead. And my preferred word, instead of "executive," is "champion." I like the word "champion." It's a label that applies to all kinds of people, including high school students and medical students—people who don't necessarily consider themselves "executives." The label expands the pool of people who may see that the ideas we're discussing about leadership are relevant to them.

Don't get caught up in these notions of what it means to be a leader and whether you're a leader. Let's instead disrupt some assumptions and myths about leadership, for example the myth that leadership has to be with a capital L, that you aren't leading if you aren't making big, transformational change. That is stifling. Leadership can have a lowercase l.

LEADERSHIP MODULE 1.C: Think Like a Social Psychologist (30 Minutes)

Video: Behavior

https://www.youtube.com/watch?v=fIk-4vt-V4g

Video transcript:

I'm a social psychologist, and I believe that social psychology is the most useful discipline for executives.

Kurt Lewin is the founding father of social psychology, and he has an equation that I often use in my classroom. The equation is something like this: Behavior is a function of both what's inside a person and the situation around that individual.

Oftentimes, we focus a lot on the individual or the personality or the person, but the lesson of social psychology is to understand that there's a broader environment. As executives, we have much more control over factors in people's environment or situation.

So I always tell my executives that if you want to change someone's behavior, change their situation.

The lesson of social psychology is that strong situations matter more for behavior than individual differences in personality. One of the goals of this course is to help you to think more like a social psychologist, or what Chicago Booth's Richard Thaler, who won the 2017 Nobel Prize for Economic Sciences, would call a "choice architect," a person who nudges people and creates environments and situations that move people in a more productive direction.

We typically act as though 80 to 90 percent of what we do is because of what's inside of a person. We tend to assume that someone behaves the way she does because of what's inside of her. This is what we tend to default to; this is personality psychology. Social psychology is just the opposite. As social psychologists, we try to create strong situations where a large part of people's behavior is a function of their environment.

The example that I use is this: you are all amazing, diverse, interesting, complicated people. You all have interesting characters, personality traits, attributes, and all sorts of other characteristics. Yet every one of you is behaving exactly the same way right now. Most eyes are on the teacher. Some of you are taking notes. I attempt a joke; you attempt to laugh. You're all engaging in classroom behavior because the classroom is a strong situation. You also made a choice to be here. The entire environment is designed for you to pay attention to the person standing at the front of the room.

Each of you is still individual, distinct, and interesting, but this example highlights how strong situations move everyone in their direction. You have the power to create strong situations that move people in this way. My hope is that you make choices that move people towards more productivity, meaning, and happiness. The choice is yours.

You should understand the awesome responsibility that you have to create strong situations. So, unpack this equation: Behavior is a function of both the person and the situation. The strong situation that we are in right now helps us to understand how similarly strong situations can impact individual behavior.

I hope my definition of leadership helps you articulate your own. I'm trying to help you unfreeze the labels you are using so that you can make better choices every day.

LEADERSHIP MODULE 1.D: Zero-Draft Leadership Definition (20 Minutes)

Video: What's Your Definition of Leadership?

https://www.youtube.com/watch?v=pba_hW8XM_g

Video transcript:

I started teaching leadership about a decade ago. Management was my first love. But I have to tell you, leadership has been keeping me up at night. It's just so hard. And the reason it's hard to be a teacher or student of leadership is because there's really no conceptual definition of what is leadership. There's no body of knowledge that "if you read this body of knowledge you are an expert in leadership." There's no discipline base in which leadership can be found.

I have come to my own conclusion. I have come to believe that what you need to do as a student of leadership is to develop your own point of view. So, this is what I've been trying to do.

When it comes to leadership, people will sell you anything that you are willing to buy. For the past ten years I have been reading a lot of this literature. And I've come up with my own point of view. I call that point of view Leadership Capital.

Leadership Capital is the wisdom to decide when to manage, and when to lead, together with the courage and capacity to act on your choices. For me, the most important elements of leadership are courage, capacity, wisdom, decision, and choice. It's my sincere hope that my point of view will help you in thinking about your own. Because what's important is that you come up with your point of view.

So, what's your definition of leadership?

Think about it. What is your definition of leadership?

Marvin Minsky, the father of artificial intelligence, has a great quote. He said that point of view is worth 80 IQ points. Imagine that just having an articulated point of view is worth 80 IQ points. I believe that each of us has an opportunity to develop our leadership capacity—what I call Leadership Capital—every day. And one way to improve your IQ is to develop a point of view on those leadership themes that matter most to you.

So, what's your definition of leadership?

At this point we can start to think more deeply about leadership and what it means. Here's a quote by James MacGregor Burns in *Encyclopedia of Leadership:* "I have come to see leadership, not only as a field of study, but as a master discipline."

The problem is, it's not a discipline. It can and does include almost everything. Leadership can be found in religion, history, economics, psychology, literature, journalism, and individual oral history. What Burns calls a "master discipline" is multi-disciplinary. It's everywhere and everything. So, what is it?

No one has the answer for you—except yourself. My definition of leadership will be different than yours. Try not to look for absolute answers or to other people when it comes to leadership. Start by looking into yourself.

Maybe you have a definition of leadership that you've articulated and written down. You are acting on some definition of leadership right now, whether or not you realize it. That definition might be inhibiting your choices, or it might be enabling them. But if you don't know what your definition is, you can't protect it. You can't pursue it. You can't understand it.

I'd like you to draft your definition of leadership, but just make it a "zero draft." We sometimes struggle to put words on paper due to our own expectations of what we are writing and how polished it should be. I have started using Peter Drucker's term "zero draft," the draft before the first one, as a way to take the pressure off people when they're writing. Using this notion of the "zero draft" can help us to feel more comfortable committing ideas to paper.

A draft means something that is not finished. A zero draft is the draft before the first one. Take a few minutes to answer this question: What is your definition of leadership? This is not your final definition. It's just your zero draft.

The goal is to keep helping you to determine your own definition of leadership and to legitimize that definition for you. This process involves writing different iterations as you learn and as grow.

Chapter 2 Leadership Modules

LEADERSHIP MODULE 2.A: Juxtapositions (20 Minutes)

We've talked about labels and about using the word "champion" instead of "manager" or "leader." We have been practicing replacing the nouns "manager" and "leader" with the verbs "managing" and "leading."

Now we're going to do an activity to drive home the point about leading and managing.

Jim March, in his book *The Ambiguities of Experience*, discusses why it's so hard to learn from experience. In everyday language, the word *exploitation* has a negative connotation, but he has an idea about exploitation versus exploration. In his context, exploitation isn't negative and simply means exploiting an opportunity, or doing as much as possible to extract optimal value in a productive way. There's a creative tension between exploitation and exploration, and it might help to think of exploitation as optimization while exploration refers to traveling through something or somewhere unknown.

This juxtaposition is similar to that between managing and leading. How do we extract more value from what we know in the here and now? How do we exploit our strengths? How do we exploit these opportunities? On the other hand, when do we explore? When do we leave the safety of the present and take risks to create a future that doesn't exist yet?

We talked before about stereotypes and myths and about how we have certain beliefs about leadership that can be limiting. Many people think management is less important than leadership. People sometimes say, "I'm just a manager," and it's rare for them to ever say, "I'm just a leader." But what's more important, the present or the future? What's more important, stability or change? What's more important, being here or going there? The answer is it depends. When do you need stability? When do you need change? When do you need to be here?

This activity is my attempt to put management and leadership on the same level plane. What do you associate with each of these words? In a past class, one student said that management is like a tiger and leadership is like a lion—because tigers are found in the tree-filled jungle while lions live on the plains with a view to the horizon. Another said that management is a red pen and leadership is a green pen.

Try to come up with two words that are roughly equivalent in valence—that have an equally positive connotation but capture the notion of future and present, change and stability, being here and going there. Take five minutes to do this exercise, and the more creative you are, the better. Talk to the person next to you and write answers directly in your book.

LEADERSHIP MODULE 2.B: The Map and Compass (30 Minutes)

Video: The Map and the Compass

https://www.youtube.com/watch?v=NfP-JRGHKqg

Video transcript:

It's incredibly important to understand the consequences of the labels that we use every day. For example, use of the noun leader implies that the behavior has something more to do with personality than with choice. I had a student who once said to me, "Well, I'm just a manager. Someday when I'm a leader, then I'll be able to do these other great things."

Why is it that we think that we are constrained by the labels that are used to describe who we are or what our opportunities might be?

Leadership is not better than management. Leadership isn't even more important than management. Management and leadership are different. They're both important.

When you're managing, you're in the present, you're in the here and now. The terrain is charted. The symbol is a map. You can look at the map, and you can see where a road is, you can plan a bridge. When you're managing, you're in the here and now; you are maintaining or enhancing the status quo.

I have students sometimes say to me, "You know, I really want to be a leader, but I need a vision. I know leaders need visions. Where do I get a vision?"

Well, visions come from your understanding of the present. When you're managing, when you're in the present, then you're in the here and now. Leadership is a choice that's made usually based on some dissatisfaction with the status quo. The vision comes from your unhappiness with some element of the current situation. So, for me the symbol for leadership is the compass because the terrain is uncharted. And all you can have is a sense of direction. The challenge is to know when to reach for the map, and when to reach the compass. Keep both close by.

Earlier we discussed juxtapositions, and this is another one: the map and a compass. To me, the map represents the present. It shows us territory that has been charted. But the future is uncharted terrain. You have only a sense of direction about it.

Let's say that you're an executive, and most of the time you're managing. You're staying on budget, delivering on promises, meeting expectations. You are using incentives such as reward power (the power to give people promotions and raises), coercive power (the power to deliver negative consequences and to take away positive things), and legitimate power (the power created by a title) to get people to do things.

Management is just as important as leadership. It is what provides a platform for the future. Without a solid present, you have no future. Management is noble and allows people to live their dreams, send their kids to school, travel on vacation, and do whatever is important to them. Most of the time, you are acting in the present. Trust is built in the present.

Now every once in a while, usually due to some dissatisfaction with the status quo, you'll make a choice to change the future. Sometimes external forces make you change, but other times leadership is a choice. You build trust in the present, and you use it when leading people into an unknown future.

Let's say that you have some dissatisfaction, large or small, with the present and have some vision of a better tomorrow. Sometimes students ask, "Where do I get a vision?" as though you can buy a ready-made vision off the shelf, but it comes from managing. A vision for a better tomorrow comes from a deep knowledge and understanding of the present. You believe so strongly in that vision that you're willing to go to a place that doesn't exist yet. It's hugely risky to make the choice to lead, and you don't want to make it often, because if you do, you'll wear out yourself and everyone around you.

You have to have confidence in your vision of the future, and you need people to believe in that vision and to believe in you. When you lead, you usually use expert power and referent power, not power that comes with your title but power that comes from within. I call it structural integrity.

People sometimes say, "I don't want to manage. I just want to lead. I just want to have vision and lead." Do they think leaders are hallucinating all the time? There's an idea that when you're managing, you need people's heads, and when you're leading, you need their hearts. But when you're leading, you need their heads *and* their hearts because they have to believe in you and your vision.

If you want to change something about an environment, start by changing your behavior. Do you want to change the way you think about leading and managing? Try changing how you use labels. If you have stereotypes and restrictive notions about what it means to lead, you're not only limiting your own opportunities, you're also limiting those of the people around you.

That's why it's so important to examine your definition of leadership. We will take a few minutes now to write down your first draft definition of leadership. If you haven't picked up on it yet, your book is meant to hold your hand on a journey that starts with a zero-draft definition of leadership and ends with your current, or working, definition. And that's just the definition you have at the end of your course; it's not the one you have at the end of your life. When you come back to the book, whenever in the future that might be, your definition will grow and evolve.

Write down your thoughts, which can be a sentence or paragraph. What is your definition of leadership? This is not your final definition. It's your first draft.

LEADERSHIP MODULE 2.C: The First Follower
(15 Minutes)

We're going to start with a short video about followership that brings us back to our discussion about leading and managing.

Video: The First Follower

https://www.youtube.com/watch?v=fW8amMCVAJQ

Video transcript:

If you've learned a lot about leadership and making a movement, then let's watch a movement happen start to finish in under three minutes and dissect some lessons. First, of course, a leader needs the guts to stand alone and look ridiculous. But what he's doing is so simple, it's almost instructional. This is key. You must be easy to follow!

Now here comes the first follower with a crucial role. He publicly shows everyone else how to follow. Notice how the leader embraces him as an equal, so it's not about the leader anymore—it's about them, plural.

Notice how he's calling to his friends to join in. See, it takes guts to be a first follower! You stand out, and you brave ridicule, yourself. Being a first follower is an under-appreciated form of leadership.

The first follower transforms a lone nut into a leader. If the leader is the flint, the first follower is the spark that really makes the fire. Now here's the second follower, this is a turning point, it's proof the first has done well. Now it's not a lone nut, and it's not two nuts. Three is a crowd, and a crowd is news.

A movement must be public. Make sure outsiders see more than just the leader. Everyone needs to see the followers because new followers emulate followers—not the leader.

Now here come two more people, then three more immediately. Now we've got momentum. This is the tipping point! And now we have a movement! As more people jump in, it's no longer risky. If they were on the fence before, there's no reason not to join in now they won't stand out, they won't be ridiculed, and they will be part of the in-crowd—if they hurry. Over the next minute you'll see the rest who prefer to stay part of the crowd because eventually they'd be ridiculed for not joining.

And, ladies and gentlemen, that is how a movement is made! So, let's recap what we learned. If you are a version of the shirtless dancing guy, all alone, remember the importance of nurturing your first few followers as equals, making everything clearly about the movement, not you. Be public. Be easy to follow! But the biggest lesson here . . . did you catch it?

Leadership is over-glorified. Yes, it started with the shirtless guy, and he'll get all the credit, but you saw what really happened. It was the first follower that transformed a lone nut into a leader. There is no movement without the first follower. See, we're told we all need to be leaders, but that would be ineffective. The best way to make a movement, if you really care, is to courageously follow and show others how to follow. When you find a lone nut doing something great, have the guts to be the first person to stand up and join in.

Chapter 3 Leadership Modules

LEADERSHIP MODULE 3.A: This I Believe (30 minutes)

We will meet in breakout groups to create collective wisdom from our individual "This I Believe" essays. Take turns reading your essay aloud to your group. Then take a few minutes to discuss the range of ideas presented. After all group members have read their essays and the group has discussed them, come to a consensus and write a single headline that captures the gist of the collective wisdom learned from your essays. Then we'll take some time to discuss the headlines from each group. Another way to debrief this activity is for each group to nominate one person to read their essay to the class.

LEADERSHIP MODULE 3.B: Definition of Success (20 minutes)

Start thinking about your definition of success while I tell you about research discussed in an article in *Science*. Researchers asked 20,000 people, from ages eighteen to sixty-eight, how much they had changed in the past decade and how much they thought they would change in the next one. The results suggest that regardless of how old you are, you think you've changed a lot in the last ten years, but you also think you're not going to change much moving forward.

Video: The Psychology of Future Self

https://www.ted.com/talks/dan_gilbert_the_psychology_of_your_future_self?language=en

What Professor Dan Gilbert says in this talk about the psychology of your future self is that we all have "an end-of-history illusion." We think that whatever we are now, that's who we're going to be forever. We think that we've all grown and changed a lot until this point, but now we're done changing. In truth, we underestimate the extent to which our future self will be different from our present self.

With this in mind, think about your definition of success. Think about the fact that you unfreeze, change, and refreeze throughout your life. According to Dan Gilbert and this research, we think that wherever we've refrozen now, that's who we are going to be from here on out. But the literature and research show that's not true at all. We have many choices that will affect our future self. We make choices both in the short term and over time that form our identities.

I would bet that most of us have thought at least a bit about our definition of success. What are your thoughts on success? What are your hopes? What's the essence of success for you? Please write your answer. And as I've said before, if you don't write it down, it doesn't exist.

Video: What's Your Definition of Success?

https://www.youtube.com/watch?v=o0_z5eQ2kA0

Video transcript:

In thinking about your future self, one of the things I think is really important is thinking about, what is your definition of success? You know, our behaviors, our goals, our hopes, our dreams, our aspirations . . . (all of it) really depends quite a bit on how we're thinking about who we want to become. And one of the truisms from social psychology is if you want to change your identity, you start by changing your behavior.

All this has me thinking that an important question, another perceptive question, is what's your definition of success? And this definition changes as you grow and evolve. I don't know if you've taken the time to write down your definition, if you've thought about how it evolves, how it has evolved, how it might evolve in the future, but this would be a good time to capture the gist or the essence of how you're defining success.

I'll tell you mine. I don't have a definition in writing, in words, but I have an illustration, a picture. It's a Venn diagram. So the idea is that: there are two circles. There's you and then there's others. And there's an intersection between these two circles. I don't know how big the intersection is for you. It could be very wide. It could be very narrow. But the idea is that in the circle that is "you," the arrows go in. So it's all about you, what you enjoy, what you love, what you're good at, what you want to do. It's all about you. In the circle that is "others," I think of it as the arrows go out, so they go out from the center. And that's all about what others want from you: what they'll pay you for, what you'll get status for, what the world wants from you. And it's the intersection between these two points, it's the cross hatch, which I think of as success.

Now, here's the thing. If you are too far out in the circle, that is you, I think ultimately that's unsustainable. You're in a place where it is all about you, it's what you want, it's what you desire, but there's no connection to the outside world, to what others will pay you, for what you get status for, what's durable. And ultimately, it's unsustainable. If you are too much in the circle of others, which is actually an easier place to be because, well, that's where we get success and status, and that's where we get accolades and that's where we get opportunities. And it's easy to stay in that place and to put one foot in front of the other, but ultimately, it's unfulfilling. So, if we're too much in either circle, it's either unsustainable or unfulfilling at some point and success is about the activities, the behaviors, the attempts we make to try to get to that intersection, that sweet spot. This is how I think about success. How do you think about success? And remember, in the service of your future self, if you want to change your identity, change your behavior.

I hope this time that *we* spent thinking about success will help you to think a little more deeply about what's important to you and how you want to go about creating your future self.

LEADERSHIP MODULE 3.C: Structural Integrity (30 minutes)

Video: Leadership and Skyscrapers by Professor Linda Ginzel

https://www.youtube.com/watch?v=pgyUmdCORaA

Commencement speeches are amazing opportunities to learn. Somebody is asked to give a speech—hopefully someone smart and thoughtful—and spending eleven or so minutes trying to say something that is of the utmost importance at a punctuation point in life when their words could make a real difference. Let's try writing a commencement speech. What do you think is worthy of eleven minutes?

The topic of my commencement address was about structural integrity and load-bearing assumptions—the biases and defaults that we use every day. Engineers building skyscrapers had certain assumptions, such as how thick the base of the building had to be to support the height.

Those assumptions limited how high they built. But with skyscrapers, engineers moved beyond those assumptions—they put a steel skeleton inside a building and built higher than was possible before. I love this metaphor for thinking about assumptions and defaults.

Pair up and discuss the following questions: How do we keep building on what we know? Can we turn off defaults and create better opportunities? You, too, have assumptions, but your internal framework—your values, core beliefs, essence, courage, capacity, wisdom, and choices—will determine how high you can go.

Chapter 4 Leadership Modules

LEADERSHIP MODULE 4.A: Vicarious Learning
(20 Minutes)

A former student got a new job as the executive director of a big international talent search organization, and she said, "You know what these companies are looking for? They're looking for executives who can manage ambiguity. Companies need executives who can handle and manage ambiguity, and they can't find them."

If executives out there aren't able to handle ambiguity, maybe it's because of how they were taught. Teachers give their students rubrics to follow and tell them what they want. Many executives, being very good students, learned to produce what their teachers asked for. But that didn't teach you how to manage ambiguity, only how to follow directions.

How can you learn to manage ambiguity?

By learning how to create your own structure. However simple this may sound, in practice it's uncomfortable and can create feelings of anxiety, but try instead to relabel that feeling as creative tension. The way to manage ambiguity is to create your own structure. This is how you can improve your ability to manage ambiguity: practice drafting frameworks to organize your thoughts and actions.

In this vein, some of the activities in this book are more difficult than others, including one I'm going to give you now. This activity is titled "Vicarious Learning." Some of you will ask, "What is it that you are looking for in this activity?" The answer is, *you* need to decide: what are you looking for? This may be one of the first times that an instructor has said to you, "You figure it out. What do you want to learn, and how do you want to go about learning it?"

When we talk about what you want to learn, there are two questions to ask yourself. First, how do you want to learn from your own experiences? Second, how do you want to learn from other people's experiences? We'll get to the second question later. Let's tackle the first question now.

There's something that I call the mezzo level, or the mezzanine. The basic idea is that you don't want your framework to be so concrete, specific, and limiting that it's in the weeds. And you don't want it to be so airy and up in the clouds that it's amorphous. The sweet spot is right in the middle, concrete enough to be actionable and abstract enough to be generalizable. When making a framework, and when communicating, we want to be on the mezzanine.

Video: Join Me on the Mezzanine

https://www.youtube.com/watch?v=SgFvdFPDQdU

Video transcript:

Kurt Lewin, the father of social psychology, has a great quote. It goes something like, "There's nothing so practical as a good theory." And the reason theories are practical is because they help us to create frameworks for organizing data. For example, we've thought a lot about frameworks. A framework can be a scaffolding. It can be a diagram. It can be a checklist. It can be a series of anything that helps you to organize, to capture data, and then to be able to access it more efficiently outside the situation in which it was created. So, I created a framework for helping people think about how to capture gist. Gist is a technical term. It means the core essence. What's the core essence? It's the gist of an idea, of a goal, of anything really.

Here's how it works. Here's the framework. A lot of times when we try to understand a concept or anything that's going on, we might be too concrete. We might be too much in the muck, in the weeds, too much in the details, and we can't see the forest for the trees. We can't get the gist. Another place where we might be is too abstract, too much in the clouds. My favorite kind of in-the-clouds notion is we have to align individual and corporate goals. Right, sounds good. What's it mean? Nobody knows. So, we can either be at 30,000 feet, which is way too high for understanding, or really in the muck, in the weeds. There's a place somewhere between these two: I call it the mezzo level. It's the sweet spot. It's the place that's just abstract enough to have meaning outside the situation where you're learning it or you're using it now. But it's concrete enough to understand how to move to action: the mezzo level.

I'm very proud of this framework. I actually created it for my students to help bring them to this sweet spot in the classroom. And my husband—who's also a psychologist, he's a cognitive psychologist—I told him about my very lovely framework. And then one day we were having one of our discussions. You might think of it as an argument, but I think of it as a discussion. And they all go something like this: he does something, and I say, "This happens, this happened last week because of this and blah, blah, blah, and then this happened, and this happens." And he looked at me at this moment and said, "Linda, would you like to join me on the mezzanine so we can solve this problem." And I said, "Yes." So, this is what happens when you marry someone smarter than you: they take your concepts and they use them against you. But he was right. He was right that I tend to default at a very concrete level and that makes it hard for people to understand gist. So, if you, wherever you default, if you default too abstract or too concrete, if you can bring it to that sweet spot, if you can get to the mezzanine, then that's the place where concepts will be most useful to generalize outside that situation.

And once you get to gist, you can turn your knowledge into action at the individual-interpersonal level, at the group or team level, and at the organizational or societal level. And the reason this concept is so important is because this isn't just about work. At the individual interpersonal level, it's about you and your partner, your spouse. At the team level it's your family. And at the organizational or societal level, it's your community, your place of worship. So frameworks, organizing data, getting to gist, communicating it . . . there's nothing so practical as a good theory.

A Vicarious Learning framework is a useful tool and asks, "What do you want to learn, and how might you go about doing that?" I'll show you an example, which was designed as a worksheet to capture what this student thought was most important in learning from a keynote speaker and other speeches. Her framework won't necessarily inform yours because you will create a framework that addresses your own specific goal in a way that works for you. There's no one right way to create a framework, and your task is to figure out what makes sense to you. Again, my guess is no one has ever asked you to do this kind of assignment before, and the main things to figure out are what you want to learn and how you are going to structure data and knowledge in order to best learn from them. Here are three pithy questions to get you started:

1. **FOCUS of your framework**: WHAT topic/theme/goal will you select as most useful for your learning outside the classroom? What is your goal?

2. **SCOPE of your framework:** WHAT do you consider in range vs. out of scope given your goal and the important lessons you want to learn?

3. **FORMAT/STRUCTURE of your framework:** HOW does your approach organize the data that will help link insight to action for your future self?

Write down your initial thoughts to begin drafting a Vicarious Learning framework. As you do, remember that a framework is not an essay or a story but a structure. It might help to think of it a scaffolding. It can be an outline, image, blueprint, or a series of questions. It can be a flowchart or a diagram. It's simply a structured way to organize data. It should be generalizable beyond the current context, and it should be actionable. It's something that will help you analyze data in order to guide your actions. It has to have a logical flow so that you can use the same framework again and again.

It can be interesting to see how others approach the same task. Now, get together with a person or two next to you and discuss your initial ideas for vicarious learning.

Here are a few examples from students. One student created a framework to learn how to improve his job search. Another person created a framework to learn from watching movies. Think of how much wiser you could be at a younger age if you were to extract value from some everyday activities, like watching movies. You can create a framework to extract more value from attending lectures, watching TED Talks, or reading the news. There are countless different ways to structure your own process of understanding; to be wiser, younger.

Many of the activities we do are meant to help you think about frameworks, and when we are together in the classroom, we learn to better articulate our frameworks.

Because this course is about your leadership development, we are working most often on frameworks that will help you improve your leadership capabilities. Here are some more questions for you to think about: What is the enduring value that emboldens you to step up and choose leadership? What are the values that you hold? What's your identity? What in your life is worth protecting? What in your life is non-negotiable?

LEADERSHIP MODULE 4.B: Public Lectures and Speeches (30 Minutes)

Video: The Surprising Science of Happiness

https://www.ted.com/talks/dan_gilbert_the_surprising_science_of_happiness?language=en

What was the most interesting thing you learned about happiness from Dan Gilbert's TED Talk? What surprised you? What are you still thinking about? Get together with a partner and discuss what you learned about happiness and what you can do to be happier.

LEADERSHIP MODULE 4.C: Leadership at the Movies (30 Minutes)

Let's talk about gist—what it is, how to extract it, how to use it to manage ambiguity.

I already pointed out that you can learn from everyday experiences. You can pay to go to a movie and spend your time there simply enjoying the show. Alternatively, you can extract more value from the experience and learn something important about yourself and about leadership. It just takes a little time and structure to do this—which will also help you be wiser, younger. And while I have opened our discussion with this mention of movies, you can practice extracting value from most anything.

You do this by capturing the gist of something, and one way to capture gist is to create your own Top 10 list. David Letterman, a late-night TV host for thirty-five years, was famous for his Top 10 lists. Each had a particular theme and was presented from 10 to 1, in reverse order of importance. You can use this same idea to capture the core essence of what you have learned. For example, you could list the top 10 books you have read in order of how much impact each has had on your growth and personal development. This seemingly simple exercise forces you to think in a pithy way about what you have learned from each book.

It's possible to teach a leadership class using only movies, without any case studies. Students can watch movies outside of class, then answer accompanying discussion questions, read supplemental material, and get together for an in-class lesson that ties together the important themes. But you don't need a teacher to do this—you can do it on your own.

There are three movies I often assign for discussion in relation to frameworks. One is *Rashomon*, which is a famous silent, black-and-white Japanese film about identity and self. The second is *Invictus*, which is about Nelson Mandela and the overturning of apartheid. The third is *Temple Grandin*, a biopic about a woman who is differently abled. This movie provides an example of harnessing the energy and value of people who break the mold.

But there are so many movies that you can learn from. *Apollo 13* is about teams, crisis, and action. You don't need to come to a classroom to learn about leadership; just watch movies with a framework in hand — create your own framework that captures the gist from your own point of view.

Because I love movies, I often use them as a learning tool. I particularly love a little clip that's posted on YouTube called *Reel Wisdom*. While watching, make note of the big themes you notice.

Video: *Reel Wisdom*

https://www.youtube.com/watch?v=l772MeHPoLM

Video transcript:

"I don't want you to think of this as just a film. Some process of converting electrons and magnetic impulses into shapes and figures and sounds. No. Listen to me."

"Shut up, listen, and learn."

"Remember, all I'm offering is the truth, nothing more."

"You are fully capable of deciding your own destiny. The question you face is which path will you choose?"

"Everything you do in life, every choice you make, has a consequence. And when you do things without thinking, you ain't making the choice, the choice is making you."

"It is not our abilities that show what we truly are. It is our choices."

"You are what you choose to be. You choose!"

"This is something only you can decide."

"No lifeguards watching anymore. You're on your own. You're your own man, and the decisions you make now are yours and yours alone from here until the end."

"I guess it comes down to a simple choice really. Get busy living or get busy dying."

"Everything that has a beginning has an end."

"But believe it or not, each and every one of us in this room is one day going to stop breathing, turn cold, and die."

"It is simply a matter of time."

"Death smiles at us all. All a man can do is smile back."

"Because we're mortal, because any moment might be our last, everything's more beautiful because we're doomed. You will never be lovelier than you are now. We will never be here again."

"Death is a natural part of life. Rejoice for those around you who transform into the force."

"Nothing ever truly dies. The universe wastes nothing. Everything is simply transformed."

"Our lives are streams, flowing into the same river."

"And so we are all connected in the great circle of life."

"Don't you be afraid sweetheart. Death is just a part of life. Something we are all destined to do."

"You cannot escape your destiny."

"Train yourself to let go of everything you fear to lose."

"Life is a box of chocolates, Forrest. You never know what you're gonna get."

"Life moves pretty fast. If you don't stop and look around once in a while, you could miss it."

"Our lives are defined by opportunities. Even the ones we miss."

"This is the way things are. You can't change nature." "Change is nature, Dad, the part that we can influence. And it starts when we decide."

"The future is not set. There is no fate but what we make for ourselves."

"No fate. No fate but what we make."

"Two little mice fell into a bucket of cream. The first mouse quickly gave up and drowned, but the second Mouse—he struggled so hard that he eventually churned that cream into butter and he walked out."

"Size matters not. Look at me. Judge me by my size, do you? Hmm? Hmm. And well you should not. For my ally is the force and a powerful ally it is. Life creates it, makes it grow. Its energy surrounds us and binds us. Luminous beings are we, not this crude matter."

"This force will be with you, always."

"But beware of the dark side. Anger, fear, aggression. The dark side of the force are they. Easily they flow, quick to join you in a fight. Once you start down the dark path, forever will it dominate your destiny, consume you it will!"

"Don't give into hate. That leads to the dark side."

"Your anger gives you great power. But if you let it, it will destroy you."

"Always remember: your focus determines your reality."

"Begin each day as if it were on purpose."

"Without purpose, we would not exist."

"Don't ever let somebody tell you that you can't do something. You got a dream, you got to protect it. People can't do something themselves, they wanna tell you, you can't do it. You want something, go get it. Period."

"You don't just live in life. You change it. You shape it. You make your mark upon it."

"What I'm talking about is the human spirit. That's the challenge, that's the voyage, that's the expedition."

"Be all you can be."

"The powerful play goes on and you may contribute a verse. What will your verse be?"

"You must strive to find your own voice, but the longer you wait to begin, the less likely you are to find it at all. Thoreau said most men lead lives of quiet desperation. Don't be resigned to that. Break out!"

"It's not about being rational, it's about following your heart."

"You must be imaginative, strong hearted. You must try things may not work. And you must not let anyone define your limits because of where you come from."

"If you focus on what you've left behind, you will never be able to see what lies ahead."

"Never look back, darling. It distracts from the now."

"Regrets are a waste of time. They're the past crippling you in the present."

"Patience!"

"When you learn to quiet your mind. You will know when you are calm, at peace. Passive."

"Your mind is like this water, my friend. When it is agitated, it becomes difficult to see. But if you allow it to settle, the answer becomes clear."

"Be whoever you want to be."

"But you're never gonna be the same person you are right now."

"So my advice to you is to get it right this time around, because this time is all you have."

"Find the joy in your life."

"All right, I'll give it a try." "No! Try not. Do. Or do not. There is no try."

"Take a deep breath. You only need one shot. Make it count."

This is just a seven-minute film, and it touches on a number of high-level, leadership themes. Let's say you have to decide what to focus on and can pick only one theme that is important to you. How do you select it? This film allows you to take a quick tour, then decide what's worthy of your time and attention.

Let me give you an example that illustrates the importance of learning from an experience, be it a movie or, in this case, a lecture. Let's say that I will give a lecture in class, then you'll be quizzed on the material. But as will be determined by a coin flip, half of you will take notes by hand, and the other half will use a laptop or device to do so.

Some research has shown that the people who take notes by hand will do statistically, significantly better on the exam than those who takes notes on their device. Those of you using a device will likely have a better record of exactly what I say because you'll be able to type quickly and capture more of the lecture. But those who write will be forced to distill and process the information I share. You'll have to record the gist of what you hear. This is the difference between awareness and understanding. You can collect a lot of knowledge, but do you understand it? And once you have it, what do you do with it? This is an example of what it means, and how important it is, to capture the gist of something for yourself.

LEADERSHIP MODULE 4.D: Best Advice (15 minutes)

Get together with a partner or two and talk about the best advice you ever received. Then select one piece of advice that your group wants to contribute to the collective class wisdom.

Maybe someone told you to assume the best in others, be yourself, own your failures, or share the rewards of success. Your group might decide to share that, or to share a different point that grows out of your individual contributions. There is so much wisdom in great advice. As a class, let's create a written compilation of our best advice.

Chapter 5 Leadership Modules

LEADERSHIP MODULE 5.A: Recent Leadership Story (15 Minutes)

When do you choose to lead? Earlier in this class, we recorded our earliest leadership experiences as a way of beginning to answer this question. Now I want you to I want you to recall and describe a more recent leadership experience. You'll have three minutes to write about it, then seven minutes to share what you wrote with your partner.

What is the enduring value that emboldened you to step up and choose leadership? This question can be difficult to answer because it's abstract, and this activity is intended to help you to unearth the answer. I want you to discover, articulate, harness, and use that knowledge. Find the link between your earliest and more recent leadership experience. What is the thread that ties them?

LEADERSHIP MODULE 5.B: Life Lessons (30 Minutes)

The title of every chapter in *Choosing Leadership* begins with an action such as writing, defining, understanding, or learning. Knowledge is necessary but not sufficient. What we want to do is move from knowledge to action.

This is not easy to do, and a lot in this book is hard. Not everybody is ready to take a deep dive into the self. But whenever you learn something new, or hear someone say something interesting, you have to capture your own understanding of it. What you take away from it may be completely different from what the next person does. And as I keep saying, be sure to take notes because if you don't write it down, it doesn't exist.

When it comes to learning, questions can be more important than the answers. Questions are tools that generalize across time and across place, and even across your own sense of self. Your answers might change over time. Right now, you may have one sense of your identity, or of how much you're willing to protect what you believe. Next year, you might have a different sense of these things.

We're going to do another activity, which involves five minutes of individual reflection. I'll give you several questions, and you pick one to answer.

Option 1: What defining moments or crucible experiences have pushed you outside your comfort zone?

Option 2: How would you complete the sentence: "I wouldn't be here now if . . . "? You can frame that in lots of ways. Maybe, "I wouldn't be now here in this classroom if..." or "I wouldn't be here in this job if," or "I wouldn't have this family if . . . " However, you'd like to frame the question is up to you.

Option 3: What five events have shaped your life?

Option 4: Draw a line on a sheet of paper from your first memory to today. Then draw another line that represents your future. Think about what moments defined your lifeline from the past and what you anticipate will define your lifeline in the future.

Now reflect on what you wrote. What was important about the experience or experiences you recorded? What was important enough to articulate and save as data? How does what you wrote tie in to who you are and where you're headed? Get together with a person or two next to you to discuss what you wrote.

Whichever question-activity you did, you can return to the others later. All of the questions share an underlying principle. Remember that the book is here for you, a companion to return to at some future date.

Chapter 6 Leadership Modules

LEADERSHIP MODULE 6.A: Counting Fs (30 Minutes)

In just a moment, we are going to do an individual task, which means I will ask you to complete it without assistance from your neighbors. We will have time to chat about the task together a little bit later, but for now you should do task this individually.

Please count the number of times that the letter F appears on the little block of text in front of you. When you're finished, you can just close the book.

Let's go ahead and collect data with a show of hands. I'd like you to just raise your hand when I get to the number of the Fs you counted.

How many people had two Fs? Three Fs? Four Fs? Five Fs? Six Fs? Seven Fs?

Before we continue with the demonstration, let me say a few words about legitimate power. We have already talked about some of the different types of power that people have. Expert and referent power come from within. Reward and coercive power, like legitimate power, come with your title. Say you're the boss, and when you ask someone to do something, you have this prerogative because you're the boss. The person you're talking to may not understand exactly why you want them to do what you've asked, but you're the boss and they do it because of the legitimate power conferred by your position.

I know that people do not tend to carry cash around with them anymore, but I'd like someone in this classroom to give me $5 from their wallet. Someone probably will because I, the teacher of this course, am here in front of all of you making this request. And there must be a legitimate reason for my needing a $5 bill, right? I must be asking for the money because I have some pedagogical purpose. This is an example of legitimate power, the kind that comes with your title.

Now I'm going to evoke my legitimate power and ask you to once again count the number of times the letter F appears on that little block of text in front of you. F as in Friday, F as in fun, F as in fantastic. Count the Fs.

Once again I'll record the numbers, I'm asking for a show of hands. How many of you had two Fs? Three Fs? Four Fs? Five Fs? Six Fs? Seven Fs?

Let's do this one more time. Count the Fs. Let's do a show of hands again.

Okay, that's it. We've got the data.

The first thing we have to do is agree that this data is veridical. I did my best to count accurately. Can we all agree that these three sets of numbers represent what we observed?

So, what did we observe? What happened over time? Every time I do this activity, the number of people reporting three Fs goes down over time, and the number of people reporting six Fs goes up. The pattern is so strong that we don't even need statistics to know that it is a significant reversal from time one to time three.

Why does this always happen? What does it mean? This is what we're always asking ourselves. We're always trying to speculate on the cause of a pattern that we observe, in our own behavior and the behavior of others.

Remember that we are all "normal neurotics," which means we all have a relatively high sense of self. We're successful and capable, and we tend to go around trying to maintain or enhance our sense of self. We do this automatically, by default. As normal neurotics, we have a variety of biases that might be getting in the way of our being wiser, younger. This is one of the demonstrations that I use to help us to think about those.

For example, we think we're right more often than we are. In psychology, this is called *overconfidence bias*. It's an example of what I call a normal neurotic bias.

Say one student thinks the answer is A. And a second student agrees. So, the first student thinks the second one is pretty smart because they both know what they think is the right answer. We automatically seek evidence that confirms our preconceived hypothesis, and this is called *confirmation bias*. As normal neurotics, we know we're right because we're smart and capable, and we want to maintain or enhance our sense of self.

One way to check this bias is to try to prove yourself wrong. You can't question yourself all the time, but you can seek disconfirming evidence, and you can only benefit by trying to prove yourself wrong. There are only two options: either you are right, or you are wrong. If you find that you are wrong, it's great you discovered this before something bad happened. And if you end up not being able to prove yourself wrong, now you can be even more certain that you were right to begin with.

There's also something called *hindsight bias*. This is when you look back on something and say, "I knew that. I knew that was going to happen all along." Did you really? Maybe, but this bias might lead you astray and can get in the way of your learning. The only way we can really check *hindsight bias,* or any of these biases, is to record data and compare it to our predictions. If we don't have accurate data, we can't use it as feedback. We can't write down and record everything, so we have to be selective about what data we capture in writing.

What do you think accounted for your behavior during this exercise? What do you think accounts for the pattern that we observed?

Very often, people answer this question by talking about how they went about finding and missing the Fs, which makes sense because the demonstration is about counting Fs. But remember the mezzanine. When dealing with demonstrations, cases, or examples, if you are too anchored in the details, you're in the weeds. You don't understand the larger lesson and need to come up one level. And if you find yourself flying at 30,000 feet, come down a little bit. Let's meet at the sweet spot, the mezzanine.

The fact that this particular demonstration is about counting Fs isn't actually important. In a few minutes no one is going to care about Fs. But how you go about completing a task can be generalized outside of this specific example. You can apply understandings to the individual, yourself; to the space between people, teams; and to groups, organizations, and society. Everything you learn—in this one task, and beyond it, especially in social psychology—can apply to both the personal and professional.

There were six Fs. <u>F</u>INISHED, <u>F</u>ILES, SCIENTI<u>F</u>-IC and three Fs in O<u>F.</u>

I didn't ask you to read, I asked you to count, and I asked this three times. But you are very good readers, and when you read for comprehension, you only see 70 percent of the text. Thirty percent is essentially invisible. You skip the text that doesn't matter for meaning, including those little connector words: if, and, or, of.

To the people who counted three Fs three times, you are the top readers in this room! You are excellent readers. You aced standardized tests for reading comprehension, and when you see a block of text, you read for meaning. This has always worked for you, and it's a default that has proven to be a great habit. It has served you well, until now.

You all have amazing habits. You're all great normal neurotics and successful people, and you would do fine in life even if you had never met me. But I can help you to be wiser, younger. Here in this classroom, we have the opportunity to experiment and collect data. Be open to these kinds of learning experiences. We have the chance to make some mistakes together and process the lessons of our experience. Doing all this will help you to improve your future outcomes. The way that you can succeed in this task is also the way you can succeed in this classroom and, beyond it, in life: turn off the default and make a different choice.

Some people use what I call the "brute force" approach. They do not read. They decide to count, but they put all their energy into not reading. They ball up their fists, brace themselves, and repeat, "I WILL NOT READ, I WILL NOT READ." These people often miss one F, or two, or all three in "of." You can take this approach, but it's often wasted time and energy.

All you need to do to ace this task is to turn off your default. This is what professional proofreaders sometimes do—they start looking at letters from the end of the sentence, and they move forward from right to left. This strategy interrupts reading without a ton of effort. It's a small change in your behavior. Don't fool yourself into thinking you have to make a big change to have a big outcome. Small changes can lead to big outcomes in your future behavior.

Video: The Ginzel Frontier

https://www.youtube.com/watch?v=gsdtHYaITGM

Video transcript:

There's an important concept in negotiations; it's called the Pareto frontier.

The Pareto frontier is that point at which maximum value from a deal is had. For example, if you don't hit the frontier in a negotiation, then you quite literally leave money on the table.

I have taken this notion and created a pseudo—another frontier. I call it the Ginzel frontier. And similar to the Pareto frontier, if you don't hit the frontier, then you quite literally leave money on the table.

But this frontier is your ability to extract lessons from your everyday experiences. To the extent that you don't collect data, experiment, practice, and reflect on your understanding of your experiences, then you leave money on the table. Your experiences are literally expensive.

Benjamin Franklin is often misquoted. People think that his quote is something like "experience is the best teacher." You've probably heard that, right? That's not his quote. What Benjamin Franklin said is that "Experience is a dear teacher, a dear teacher." It's expensive.

And you know why experiences are expensive? Because we don't learn from them. Just because we have a success or a failure, it doesn't mean we learned anything from it or, or maybe we learned the wrong things from it.

So, what I try to do is to help people to be more systematic in collecting the data of their experience. And the way to do that is to experiment, to practice across time, experiment with your behavior. Practice across time, collect data, feedback, and reflect on that data.

Maybe you think about data just as feedback. Okay. So just think how fortunate you are, if you have a boss who gives you feedback, or a spouse, or if you're like me and you have a teenage son who tells you everything you do wrong on a moment-by-moment basis. To the extent that you don't collect data, experiment, practice, and reflect on your understanding of your experiences, then you leave money on the table. Your experiences are literally expensive.

Let's take a few minutes now to read the two sections in the workbook that appear right after the Counting Fs demonstration. The main idea has to do with the link between knowledge and action. Knowledge is necessary but not sufficient. Domain knowledge is what you bring to a situation, it is the real-world knowledge—such as knowing industry standards or a company's specific operating procedures—acquired on the job. Conceptual knowledge is what I bring into the classroom, discipline-based theories from social psychology. We combine these two types of knowledge during our sessions.

Harry Davis and Robin Hogarth tell us that we need more than knowledge; we need action. Their framework highlights the importance of behavior. Action skills represent your ability to put conceptual and domain knowledge into practice to change your future behavior.

I think the two most important action skills are negotiation skills and decision-making skills. Insight skills, the practice of learning the right lessons from experience, follow closely behind. When you collect data, conduct experiments, look at trends across time, and identify your defaults, you are developing your insight skills.

LEADERSHIP MODULE 6.B Focus on Strengths (40 Minutes)

Video: Focus on Strengths

https://www.youtube.com/watch?v=W1R4R4170wQ

Video transcript:

With reference to Star Wars, every force has a light side and a dark side. And we want to move more toward the light side. Focusing on strengths, I think, is a great example of this.

It's important to not start with something you don't have; not to start with weaknesses, but to build from strengths. I teach a lot of executives, and it's interesting that they don't think about leveraging strengths as a development opportunity.

We're so focused on weaknesses and that we think that we have to help people improve their weaknesses. I encourage you to try leveraging your strengths. How about doing more of what you do well every day?

Peter Drucker, the father of modern management, urged executives to play the strengths, their own strengths, the strengths of their boss, their direct reports, their peers, even the strengths of situation around them. Making strengths productive is such an important tenet that Drucker called it a "moral imperative."

Think about it. To focus on weaknesses is not only foolish, it's irresponsible.

Drucker calls it a moral imperative to focus on strengths. He says, "To focus on weakness is not only foolish, it's irresponsible." I love this idea. Let's put this idea into action now by taking fifteen minutes to complete the online assessment, Values in Action (VIA) Character Strengths Profile: *https://www.viacharacter.org/survey/surveys/takesurvey*. Upon completing this assessment, you will receive a rank-order list of twenty-four character strengths. Your task beyond the classroom will be to use this data to leverage your strengths. You'll get together with a person or two next to you for ten minutes and discuss your answers to the question: how can you do more of what you do well every day?

It's a good idea to turn off the default of focusing on weaknesses and instead focus on what you do well. Too often, people think that you development is about identifying and addressing your weaknesses, and I'm not saying that you should ignore your weaknesses. But it's incredibly valuable to work on strengths. Do more of what you do well, as that is what can make you great.

Make focusing on strengths your default setting. I do not believe that we will ever neglect our weaknesses, but we can work to make our strengths salient. A lot of times, we take our strengths for granted because they come easily to us, but don't do that, and don't hide them. As Ben Franklin pointed out, a sundial in the shade can't tell time. You need to put your strengths in the open, not in the shadows.

LEADERSHIP MODULE 6.C: Exit Ticket (10 Minutes)

We've discussed frameworks, and there's one that was created by a student who called it Exit Ticket. He suggests that at the end of an activity, class, event, or meeting, you should ask yourself: What are three things I learned? What are two things you're going to share with others? And what's one action you will take?

You can customize this framework for your own purpose. For example, instead of three things, what are two things you learned from our "This I Believe" exercise? When it comes to a movie, why not write down one action it inspired you to take, or one experiment that it motivated you to do? The framework helps us to reinforce the lesson that it only takes a little bit of time and a little bit of structure to extract your own gist from any given experience.

This goes back to the idea of being wiser, younger. The time you spend in class can be more or less expensive, depending on how much value you extract. We have discussed insight skills and the importance of learning the right lessons from experience, and we have talked about how leadership development is as much about learning as it is about leadership. So once again, how do we extract more value from our experiences? There are endless variations you can create of the "exit ticket" framework to capture gist.

Chapter 7 Leadership Modules

LEADERSHIP MODULE 7.A: Be Wiser, Younger
(30 Minutes)

Video: Make Leadership a Verb

https://www.youtube.com/watch?v=XGNGh9FMpcg

Video transcript:

There are stereotypes associated with what it means to be a leader or what it means to be a manager. And we actually limit our choices, our own behaviors, and the behaviors of others, when we use these types of labels.

My friend and colleague Rick Larrick proposes the following challenge to his students, and I have adopted this challenge. Try, in your everyday conversations, in your everyday language, to use the words lead *and* manage *as verbs, as opposed to using the words* leadership *and* management *as nouns.*

If you think about the fact that everyone can engage in leadership behavior independent of personality traits or position in an organization, then you can understand the power that comes from using lead and manage as verbs as opposed to assuming that they are people or positions.

When we start to understand leading and managing are behaviors—and that we can choose to engage in the behaviors of leading and managing, then this really allows us to practice leadership more often and it allows us to create an environment that helps other people to develop their leadership capital. And so that's the homework assignment; you'll see that it's harder than you think.

When I read this Alinsky quote, I thought, *This is why we don't learn from our experiences. Because we're not even having experiences! We're having happenings that pass through our system undigested.*

Only if we process and digest lessons might they become experiences from which we might learn something. This is why everyone who grows old is not wise. We do not gain knowledge just by having happenings. We have to digest it, then ask, "What did I learn? What will I do differently?" We capture that and write it down to extract the value.

Misbehaving is Richard Thaler's first-person narrative of the making of behavioral economics. Here's what Professor Thaler tells us we should do.

This comes from the section about the importance of collecting data on pages 355–356 of *Misbehaving*:

> Collect data. Stories are powerful and memorable. That's why I've told so many in this book ... But an individual anecdote can only serve as an illustration. To really convince yourself, much less others, we need data. We need to change the way we do things. We need data, and lots of it. As Mark Twain once said, "It ain't what you don't know that gets you into trouble, it's what you know for sure that just ain't so."
>
> People become over-confident because they never bother to document their past track record of wrong predictions, and then they make things worse by falling victim to the dread confirmation bias. They only look for evidence that confirms their pre-conceived hypothesis. The only protection against over-confidence and these other biases, defaults, heuristics . . . is to systematically collect data, especially data that can prove you wrong. As my Chicago colleague Linda Ginzel always tells her students, "If you don't write it down, it doesn't exist."

This is why it's so important to collect the data of your experience. We have defaults, which are biases, shortcuts, and heuristics. To be wiser, younger, and to make better choices in the future, you want to identify your defaults, practice turning them off, and make better choices. There are lots of ways to identify defaults. You can get feedback from someone else, or you can recognize on your own that you want to turn off a default.

We discussed doing experiments in your life, and this is what you can do every time you make a different choice. Change your behavior and see what happens. Collect that data across time. This is how you learn directly from your own experience. What default do you want to turn off, and what do you want to work on?

LEADERSHIP MODULE 7.B: Leadership Myth Busting (25 Minutes)

Marvin Minsky, the father of artificial intelligence, said that point of view is worth 80 IQ points. This is a great quote. There are N people in this room. We can raise the IQ in this room by N x 80 = 80N IQ points. That's pretty amazing. This is the goal, to help you develop your point of view around leadership and around what matters to you—not around what matters to me, and not around what matters to other people, but what matters to *you*. What are the themes in your life that are most relevant for you?

This class is based on the idea that students can learn to use the knowledge of social psychology. Recall that social psychology is the branch of psychology that deals with the social environment—the situations in which we find ourselves where people influence and are influenced by others.

Social psychology is *not* about teaching management how to manipulate or use people. It's about making decisions that will create strong environments and move people, including yourself, in a more productive direction. Social psychology can help us do this.

Professor Thaler would call you "choice architects." You make choices to "nudge" people in various social environments. He's actually talking about how you can put social psychology into action.

Unfortunately, few people in the leadership industry recognize this. They rely on the personality-based view of leadership we discussed earlier and on all kinds of unhelpful leadership myths that constrain us. Is the prototypical a leader a man? Attractive? Tall? Handsome? Of a certain age? Does he have certain credentials?

Some people think leaders are born with charisma. They think that leaders are all extroverted and that introverted people can't lead, or that leadership is based on seniority. These are stereotypes.

But are we saying that people who don't fit these descriptions haven't led? It's not true. We have all engaged in leadership behaviors. Please turn to page 129 and spend a few minutes on this exercise.

There are a lot of myths and stereotypes around leadership, and we're going to attack some of these. A lot of people think leadership happens only at the C-suite level, at a top level with a top-level authority. But what does this mean? How much do you have to be paid to be considered a leader? And how is a leader different from a manager? How are you thinking about this? Whatever your definition of what it means to be a leader, it's affecting your behavior, whether you recognize it or not.

LEADERSHIP MODULE 7.C: The Zeigarnik Effect (20 Minutes)

Video: The Zeigarnik Effect

https://www.youtube.com/watch?v=Z_Hs_0Qiv0U

Video transcript:

If you've ever had a problem or situation that you're working to resolve, and you're not really thinking about it consciously at the moment, but you're in the shower, and all of a sudden, an idea comes to you. Or you go to sleep, and you wake up, or even in the middle of the night, and you have an idea about something that's been bothering you, something you've been working on. That is the Zeigarnik effect.

I'm going to introduce you to Bluma Zeigarnik. Bluma was a psychologist, and she's responsible for identifying the Zeigarnik effect, the tendency to remember incomplete tasks better than completed ones.

Ernest Hemingway is said to have used the Zeigarnik effect to his advantage. He would end each day of his writing by stopping mid-sentence. Instead of completing his thought, he would allow the Zeigarnik effect, this productive tension, to work for him.

Executives tend to rush to closure. We have a bias for action. We want to move on and get the answer so that we can get a lot of things done. But I always say that perceptive questions are much more important than answers. And this is because questions are tools.

Questions generalize across time and place, whereas answers are specific to a given context. It's my hope that you will practice staying in the question where creativity and energy often reside, along with uncertainty and anxiety.

May Zeigarnik be with you.

Let's talk about the Zeigarnik effect, the tendency to remember unfinished tasks more than completed tasks. In class, we tend to leave things unfinished, then come back and pick them up again after some time has passed so that Zeigarnik can be with you.

We have talked about managing ambiguity and started to think about creating a framework for learning from the experience of others. I know that this is a difficult task because we aren't usually asked to deal with ambiguity and to create structure in this way. But another way that we can get more comfortable with ambiguity is to practice staying in the question.

Everyone wants closure. We tend to rush to an answer and have a bias for action, which has a light side and a dark side. The advantage is you get a lot done, but if we can stay in the question—where there's uncertainty, and even anxiety—there can be a productive tension that fuels ideas and actions. That is another way that we can manage ambiguity. Skills benefit from practice, and staying in the question is a skill that can benefit from practice. Practice not rushing to closure. Practice this while you're here in the classroom, where it is safe to take risks.

In *Choosing Leadership* you have opportunities to practice both letting Zeigarnik be with you and coming to some kind of closure, but the closure should link to action. The idea is to help you to become your own coach, your own professor for life. Coach yourself, provide feedback, and you'll be your own advocate for your future self and for being more present about who you want to become. You're going to change. Are you changing in a way that is moving you toward the hopes you have for yourself? Let's take another step together in our leadership journey and practice individual written reflection plus collective wisdom with the "Three Questions." Let's turn to pages 136–137.

ACKNOWLEDGMENTS:
REVISED AND EXPANDED EDITION

> **Well done is better than well said.**
> —Benjamin Franklin

irst and foremost, loving gratitude goes to my husband and sons who are my biggest champions.

It has been four years since the publication of the original workbook, and I owe a million thanks to those people who have helped me to seed the grassroots leadership development movement that is *Choosing Leadership*. Special thanks to Tomer Keysar, my favorite filmmaker, who created the new instructional videos for the learning modules; web guru Sam Giberson, who designed both the websites ChoosingLeadershipBook.com and BeWiserYounger.com; Kevin Bendle, my all-time favorite bookseller; and Carmen Marti, whose writing brought *Choosing Leadership* to a variety of audiences.

Special thanks go to the Booth MBA students who studied these ideas and taught me how to think about leadership even more complexly than

I could have imagined during the last four years. They include executive MBA students in London, cohorts EXP-24 through EXP-27; in Hong Kong, AXP-18 through AXP-21; and in Chicago, XP-88 through XP-91. Also, full-time and evening/weekend students who took Leadership Capital and Leadership at the Movies when I first introduced these courses into the Booth curriculum during the summer and fall of 2021.

My little picture book, *Leadership Is . . .* , started as a post-class Zoom conversation with my EMBA students and their children, and thanks to illustrator Katie Harris, project manager Katelyn Wang, and dozens of volunteers around the world who translated this little book into more than thirty languages, it has become a community effort to change the global conversation around leadership for young children. You can participate by downloading free, multilingual PDFs here: choosingleadershipbook.com/little-champions.

It was a unique privilege to introduce my Booth leadership course into the undergraduate curriculum at the University of Chicago. With special fondness, I will always remember the pioneering students who were among the first college students to take my Choosing Leadership course in the winters of 2021 and 2022. And as for helping high school students to be wiser, younger, my thanks go to James Nandorf, my favorite VP and Dean of Admissions at the University of Chicago. He provided me the opportunity to bring *Choosing Leadership* to my youngest group of students both in the United States through the Trott Emerging Rural Leaders Program and globally through Rise, an initiative of Schmidt Futures and the Rhodes Trust.

My amazing teaching assistants span the range from undergraduate teaching interns to senior staff at the Booth School of Business, with thanks, in alphabetical order: Zeynep Aslan, Bryan Baird, Lisbeth Brillant, Amanda Gecht, Jack Goodkin, Leigh Grant, Jason Kowalski, Carmen Marti, Kenneth Onishi, Matthew Ramoundos, Rebecca White, Blakely Winstead, and Stephanie Wisner.

And, continuing my long-term tradition of mentoring the sisters of AOPi, I would like to recognize the University of Chicago undergraduates who have served as research assistants since 2019, Kelly Han, Ally Kong, Mia Yu, and Katelyn Wang.

It is important for me to thank a handful of amazing people who contributed their time and talent to creating the revised and expanded edition of *Choosing Leadership*. First, of course, is Emily Lambert who continues to work her editorial magic and always makes my writing better. Char Bennington whose insight and expertise led to the formatting of the Leadership Modules as Part 2 and thus created a truly hybrid book demonstrating how we learn with one hand and teach with the other. Kelly Han who transcribed the videos and formatted the Leadership Modules while managing the tightest of deadlines with the utmost grace. Finally, to Les Ford and Shanna Horvatin for teaching me that my being assigned the middle seat on an airplane can be a tremendous opportunity for community building. My best wishes to the pirate and his bride!

They say "it takes a village," and I know it to be true for this expanded and revised workbook is the product of such a village. My gratitude story begins with Katie Harris, the incomparable illustrator of *Leadership Is . . .* , who was among my first undergraduate leadership students where she put her artistic talents to academic purpose. Katie introduced me to "The Obi-Wan Kenobi of Publishing," Mr. Robert Solomon, Esquire, who introduced me to Mr. Christian Blonshine and my new publisher, Health Communications, Inc. Then, a miracle occurs here. And I have the privilege to work with Christine Belleris, Editorial Director par excellence. Together with Lindsey Mach, PR and Marketing maven, they are champions for *Choosing Leadership: Revised and Expanded.*

We are never going to be younger than we are today, but we can be wiser tomorrow. The earlier we break leadership stereotypes, the better. Thanks to all of you who are creating a better future where people everywhere have the courage, capacity, and wisdom to make leadership a choice.

ACKNOWLEDGMENTS:
FIRST EDITION

> ## " The long road knows the horse's strength.
> —CHINESE PROVERB AS TOLD TO ME BY REIKO HASUIKE IN 1985

I owe a special debt of gratitude to the two most influential teachers in my life, both experimental social psychologists, Gary Stern and Ned Jones, in memory. And I want to honor a special collection of people who I have looked up to as friends and mentors on my own journey of lifelong learning, beginning at the University of Colorado, then moving to Princeton, Stanford, and Northwestern, before settling at the University of Chicago: Daniel Gilbert; Harold Leavitt, in memory; Max Bazerman; Jeffrey Pfeffer; Harry Davis; Robin Hogarth; Howard Haas, in memory; and Richard Thaler.

I am privileged to be on this long road with Boaz Keysar, Jonathan Eig, Barbara Passy, and my children Ely, Tomer, and Avi. Boaz is my husband and my biggest champion. Jonathan is my favorite *New York Times* bestselling biographer, and I am grateful for his friendship, encouragement, and advice. Barbara continues to influence my choices through her tenacious support of my ideas and overconfidence in my ability. The positive impact that they have is equal in strength and in direct opposition to the negative impact of he who must not be named.

It is important for me to thank a handful of amazing people who contributed to the development of the original book for my MBA course, *Leadership Capital*, which served as model for *Choosing Leadership*. First and foremost, Emily Lambert worked her editorial magic by turning my lecture notes into prose; Joseph Colitto inspired me to make my text worthy of his beautiful design, including his breathtaking image of the green pen for this book; Molly Heim elevated the stature of proofreading to previously unimaginable heights; Daniel Lozano graciously provided feedback from the student perspective and encouraged me to consider wider distribution of these ideas. And to Nicole Rotunda who has chosen to dedicate her considerable talent and energy to bring these ideas to the world outside my classroom.

I would like to recognize the University of Chicago undergraduates who have served as research assistants, notably the sisters of AOPi, Suzanne Adatto, Brittany Agostino, Evaline Bai, Katherine Haselkorn, June Huang, Priyanka Mehta, Justyna Nytko, Kathleen Oliver, Sunila Steephen, Patricia Tracz, and Melissa Wong. I am especially grateful to Stacy Wang, who sourced the leadership stories and created the illustrations for this book, and Sara Chan, who formatted the manuscript, treed the references, secured permissions, and generally makes everything I do better.

Booth PhD candidates, post-doctoral scholars, and MBAs who served as teaching assistants, but taught me more than I taught them, in alphabetical order: Zachary Burns, Bess Cades, Stephanie Chen, Barry Cinnamon, Avigail Goldgrabber, Dylan Hall, Sayuri Hayakawa, Hye-young Kim, Nadav Klein, Jasmine Kwong, Soraya Lambotte, Debbie Ma, Cade Massey, Alexander Moore, Juliana Schroeder, Daniel Walco, Natalie Wheeler, and Blakely Winstead. Extra special mention goes to Rebecca White, who has taught together with me across many years, courses, and continents.

Special thanks to the Booth MBA students who studied these ideas as I worked to develop the framework of Leadership Capital over the last 10 years. They include Booth Executive MBA students in London, cohorts EXP-20 through EXP-23; in Hong Kong, AXP-14 through AXP-17; and in Chicago, XP-84 through XP-87, as well as the full-time and evening/weekend MBA students who took The Practice of Leadership when I taught it from 2006 through 2014.

Kevin Bendle, my favorite book store manager, who spent many years telling me that I should write a book and then decided to take matters into his own hands and make it happen by introducing me to Agate Publishing. A simple word of thanks to their talented and dedicated staff who I had the privilege of working with, specifically Jacqueline Jarik, Deirdre Kennedy, and the amazing Morgan Krehbiel.

Finally, thanks to you for making your leadership development journey on the pages of this book. Please visit the book's website *ChoosingLeadershipBook.com* and review the video resources whenever you want a quick reminder of what you have learned. Life is a work in progress. My hope is that this book will be a worthy companion. Together, we can create a better future.

APPENDIX A: ACTIVITY INDEX

APPENDIX A: Activity Index

Activity	Page number	Date completed
Activity 1.1 Earliest Leadership Story	13	
Activity 1.2 Zero-Draft Leadership Definition	25	
Activity 2.1 Juxtaposing Leadership and Management	28	
Activity 2.2 Capital L Leadership Story	33	
Activity 2.3 What Makes You an Effective Follower?	41	
Activity 2.4 First-Draft Leadership Definition	43	
Activity 3.1 This I Believe	50	
Activity 3.2 Your Commencement Speech	63	
Activity 4.1 Vicarious-Learning Framework	71	
Activity 4.2 Your "Top 10" Framework	76	
Activity 4.3 "I have not walked alone" Framework	55	
Activity 4.4 The Best Advice	90	
Activity 5.1 Most Recent Leadership Experience	94	

APPENDIX A: Activity Index (continued)

Activity	Page number	Date completed
Activity 5.2 Lifelines, Past and Future Selves	98	
Activity 5.3 Analyzing Impact	103	
Activity 6.1 Strengths Data	118	
Activity 6.2 Exit Ticket	124	
Activity 7.1 Point of View	136	
Activity 7.2 Final Paper	140	
Activity 7.3 Current Definition of Leadership	141	

APPENDIX B: LEADERSHIP MODULE INDEX

APPENDIX B: Leadership Module Index

Activity	Page number
Leadership Module A: Building Community (30 min.)	145
Leadership Module B: Beginnings and Endings (15 min.)	147
Leadership Module C: Choosing Leadership Introduction (10 min.)	148
Leadership Module 1.A: Early Leadership Story (45 min.)	151
Leadership Module 1.B: Labels (30 min.)	154
Leadership Module 1.C: Think Like a Social Psychologist (30 min.)	156
Leadership Module 1.D: Zero-Draft Leadership Definition (20 min.)	158
Leadership Module 2.A: Juxtapositions (20 min.)	161
Leadership Module 2.B: The Map and Compass (30 min.)	162
Leadership Module 2.C: The First Follower (15 min.)	164
Leadership Module 3.A: This I Believe (30 min.)	167
Leadership Module 3.B: Definition of Success (20 min.)	167

APPENDIX B: Leadership Module Index (continued)

Activity	Page number
Leadership Module 3.C: Structural Integrity (15 min.)	169
Leadership Module 4.A: Vicarious Learning (20 min.)	171
Leadership Module 4.B: Public Lectures and Speeches (30 min.)	175
Leadership Module 4.C: Leadership at the Movies(30 min.)	175
Leadership Module 4.D: Best Advice (15 min.)	180
Leadership Module 5.A: Recent Leadership Story (15 min.)	181
Leadership Module 5.B: Life Lessons (30 min.)	181
Leadership Module 6.A: Counting Fs (30 min.)	183
Leadership Module 6.B: Focus on Strengths (40 min.)	188
Leadership Module 6.C: Exit Ticket (10 min.)	189
Leadership Module 7.A: Be Wiser, Younger (30 min.)	191
Leadership Module 7.B: Leadership Myth Busting (25 min.)	193
Leadership Module 7.C: The Zeigarnik Effect (20 min.)	194

APPENDIX C: VIDEO INDEX

APPENDIX C: Video Index

Activity	Page number
Introduction to *Choosing Leadership* (2:50) https://www.choosingleadershipbook.com/	148
Earliest Leadership Experience (4:06) https://www.youtube.com/watch?v=IS7LD0Ekym0	151
How Labels Manage Meaning (3:49) https://www.youtube.com/watch?v=hXgGM5BtxyI	154
Behavior (0:58) https://www.youtube.com/watch?v=fIk-4vt-V4g	156
What's Your Definition of Leadership? (2:40) https://www.youtube.com/watch?v=pba_hW8XM_g	158
The Map and the Compass (2:02) https://www.youtube.com/watch?v=NfP-JRGHKqg	162
The First Follower (2:57) https://www.youtube.com/watch?v=fW8amMCVAJQ	164

Activity	Page number
The Psychology of Future Self (6:36) https://www.ted.com/talks/ dan_gilbert_the_psychology_of_your_future_self?language=en	167
What's Your Definition of Success? (3:39) https://www.youtube.com/watch?v=o0_z5eQ2kA0	168
Leadership and Skyscrapers by Professor Linda Ginzel (15.04) https://www.youtube.com/watch?v=pgyUmdCORaA	169
Join Me on the Mezzanine (4:26) https://www.youtube.com/watch?v=SgFvdFPDQdU	172
The Surprising Science of Happiness (20:52) https://www.ted.com/talks/ dan_gilbert_the_surprising_science_of_happiness?language=en	175
Reel Wisdom (7:01) https://www.youtube.com/watch?v=I772MeHPoLM	176
The Ginzel Frontier (2:18) https://www.youtube.com/watch?v=gsdtHYaITGM	187
Focus on Strengths (1:15) https://www.youtube.com/watch?v=W1R4R4170wQ	188
Make Leadership a Verb (1.30) https://www.youtube.com/watch?v=XGNGh9FMpcg	191
The Zeigarnik Effect (1:42) https://www.youtube.com/watch?v=Z_Hs_0QivOU	194

CITATIONS

Alinsky, Saul D. *Rules for Radicals: A Practical Primer for Realistic Radicals.* New York: Vintage Books, 1989.

Allison, Jay, and Dan Gediman, eds. *This I Believe: The Personal Philosophies of Remarkable Men and Women.* New York: Henry Holt & Co., 2007.

Ammons, A. R. *The Really Short Poems of A. R. Ammons.* New York: W. W. Norton & Co., 1992.

Apollo 13. Directed by Ron Howard. Universal City, CA: Universal Pictures, 1995. DVD.

Badaracco Jr., Joseph L. "The Discipline Of Building Character." *Harvard Business* Review 76, no. 2 (1998): 114–124.

———. "Leadership in Literature." *Harvard Business Review* 84, no. 3 (2006): 47–55.

Balis, Tony. "Some Suggestions on Writing a Commencement Speech." *The Humanity Initiative.* http://www.humanity.org/voices/commencements/writing-commencement-speeches.

Bazerman, Max. *The Power of Noticing: What the Best Leaders See.* New York: Simon & Schuster, 2014.

Becker, Gary S. *Human Capital: A Theoretical and Empirical Analysis, with Special Reference to Education.* Chicago: University of Chicago Press, 1964; 1993.

Bennis, Warren G. *On Becoming a Leader*. New York: Basic Books, 2009.

Bennis, Warren G., and Robert J. Thomas. *Leading for a Lifetime: How Defining Moments Shape the Leaders of Today and Tomorrow*. Boston: Harvard Business Review Press, 2007.

Bradbury, Ray. *Fahrenheit 451*. New York: Ballantine Books, 1953.

Burns, James MacGregor. *Leadership*. New York: Harper & Row, 1978.

Burton, Susan. "Terry Gross and the Art of Opening Up." *The New York Times Magazine*, October 25, 2015.

Calkins, Lucy. *The Art of Teaching Reading*. New York: Longman, 2001.

Carlin, John. *Playing the Enemy: Nelson Mandela and the Game that Made a Nation*. London: Penguin Books, 2008.

Cattell, Raymond B., and Glen F. Stice. "Four Formulae for Selecting Leaders on the Basis of Personality." *Human Relations*, May 1954.

Chaleff, Ira. *The Courageous Follower: Standing Up to & for Our Leaders*. Oakland: Berrett-Koehler Publishers, 2009.

Coelho, Paulo. *The Alchemist*. New York: HarperOne, 1993.

Coutu, Diane. "Ideas As Art." *Harvard Business Review* 84, no. 10 (2006): 82–89.

Covey, Stephen R. *The 7 Habits of Highly Effective People: Powerful Lessons in Personal Change*. New York: Free Press, 2004.

Crimes and Misdemeanors. Directed by Woody Allen. Los Angeles: Orion Pictures, 1989. DVD.

Davis, Harry, and Robin M. Hogarth. "Rethinking Management Education: A View from Chicago." *Chicago Booth Selected Papers Series* 72 (1992; 2013). https://www.ChicagoBooth.edu/faculty/selected-paper-series.

Dead Poets Society. Directed by Peter Weir. Burbank, CA: Buena Vista Pictures, 1989. DVD.

Drucker, Peter F. *The Effective Executive: The Definitive Guide to Getting the Right Things Done*. New York: Harper Business, 1967; 2006.

Epley, Nicholas. *Mindwise: How We Understand What Others Think, Believe,*

Feel and Want. New York: Knopf, 2014.

Fisher, Robert, and Mary Williams, eds. *Unlocking Creativity: A Teacher's Guide to Creativity Across the Curriculum*. Abingdon, Oxon: David Fulton Publishers, 2004.

Fortune editors. "The Best Advice I Ever Got." *Fortune,* October 25, 2012. http://fortune.com/2012/10/25/the-best-advice-i-ever-got/.

Fresh Air. Hosted by Terry Gross. Produced at WHYY-FM in Philadelphia. http://www.npr.org/programs/fresh-air/.

Gardner, John W. *On Leadership*. New York: Free Press, 1990.

Garg, Sonny. "Implementing Change." Lecture, Chicago Booth, Chicago, March 6, 2014.

George, Bill, Peter Sims, Andrew N. McLean, and Diana Mayer. "Discovering Your Authentic Leadership." *Harvard Business Review* 85, no. 2 (2007): 132–8.

Gilbert, Daniel. *Stumbling on Happiness*. New York: Knopf, 2006.

Gosling, Jonathan, and Henry Mintzberg. "The Five Minds of a Manager." *Harvard Business Review* 81, no. 11 (2003): 54–63.

Grandin, Temple. *The Way I See It: A Personal Look at Autism and Asperger's*. 2nd ed. Arlington, TX: Future Horizons, 2011.

———. "The World Needs All Kinds of Minds." TED, 2010. https://www.ted.com/talks/temple_grandin_the_world_needs_all_kinds_of_minds.

Gross, Terry. *All I Did Was Ask: Conversations with Writers, Actors, Musicians, and Artists*. New York: Hyperion, 2004.

Hesse, Hermann. *The Journey to the East*. Translated by Hilda Rosner. New York: Noonday Press–Farrar, Straus & Giroux, 1969.

High Fidelity. Directed by Stephen Frears. Burbank, CA: Buena Vista Pictures, 2000. DVD.

Immelt, Jeffrey. "Things I Learned." LinkedIn, July 31, 2017. https://linkedin.com/pulse/things-i-learned-jeff-immelt/.

Invictus. Directed by Clint Eastwood. Burbank, CA: Warner Bros. Pictures, 2009. DVD.

Jobs, Steve. "2005 Stanford University Commencement Address." Speech, Stanford, CA, June 12, 2005. http://news.stanford.edu/2005/06/14/jobs-061505/.

Kalanithi, Paul. *When Breath Becomes Air*. New York: Random House, 2016.

Kellerman, Barbara. "What Every Leader Needs to Know about Followers." *Harvard Business Review* 85, no. 12 (2007): 84–9.

Kelley, Robert E. "In Praise of Followers." *Harvard Business Review* 66, no. 6 (1988): 142–148.

———. *The Power of Followership: How to Create Leaders People Want to Follow, and Followers Who Lead Themselves*. New York: Doubleday/Currency, 1992.

Kennedy, John F. "Full Text: JFK's Never-Delivered Speech from Dallas." Pittsburgh Post-Gazette, November 21, 2013 http://www.post-gazette.com/news/nation/2013/11/22 Full-text-JFK-s-never-delivered-speech-from-Dallasstories/201311210356.

King Jr., Martin Luther. "Letter from Birmingham Jail." Open letter, Birmingham, AL, April 16, 1923. https://www.africa.upenn.edu/Articles_Gen/ Letter_Birmingham.html.

Konnikova, Maria. "On Writing, Memory, and Forgetting: Socrates and Hemingway Take on Zeigarnik." Literally Psyched (blog). Scientific American. April 30, 2012. http://blogs.scientificamerican.com/literally-psyched/on-writing-memory-and-forgetting-socrates-and-hemingway-take-on-zeigarnik/.

Kotter, John P. "What Leaders Really Do." *Harvard Business Review* 68, no. 3 (1990): 103–111.

Leavitt, Harold. *Top Down: Why Hierarchies Are Here to Stay and How to Manage Them More Effectively*. Boston: Harvard Business School Press, 2005.

———. "Group Decision and Social Change." In *Readings in Social Psychology*, 340–44. New York: Henry Holt & Co., 1947.

Letterman, David. *The "Late Night with David Letterman" Book of Top Ten Lists*. New York: Pocket Books, 1990.

Lewin, Kurt, Fritz Heider, and Grace M. Heider. *Principles of Topological Psychology*. New York: McGraw-Hill, 1936.

Lewin, Kurt. "Frontiers in Group Dynamics: Concept, Method, and Reality in Social Science; Social Equilibria and Social Change." *Human Relations*, 1947.

Lewis, Randy. "Inspiring a Vision." Lecture, Chicago Booth, Chicago, February 20, 2014.

March, James G. *The Ambiguities of Experience*. Ithaca: Cornell University Press, 2010.

McNulty, Eric J. "Leadership Development's Epic Fail." MITSloan Management Review , May 1, 2017.

———."Forget the Resolutions—Write Your Personal Manifesto." Strategy+Business (blog). December 21, 2016. https://www.strategy-business.com/blog/Forget-the-Resolutions-Write-Your-Personal-Manifesto?gko=d24dc.

Minnow, Nell. *The Movie Mom's Guide to Family Movies*. 2nd edition. Bloomington: iUniverse, 2004.

Muth, John J. *The Three Questions: Based on a Story by Leo Tolstoy*. New York: Scholastic Press, 2002.

Pausch, Randy. "Randy Pausch Last Lecture: Achieving Your Childhood Dreams." Speech, Pittsburgh, PA, December 20, 2007. https://www.youtube.com/watch?v=ji5_MqicxSo.

———. *The Last Lecture*. New York: Hyperion, 2008.

Pfeffer, Jeffrey. *Leadership BS: Fixing Workplaces and Careers One Truth at a Time*. New York: Harper Business, 2015.

———. *Power: Why Some People Have It and Others Don't*. New York: HarperCollins, 2010.

Rashomon. Directed by Akira Kurosawa. New York: Criterion Collection, 1950. DVD.

"Reel Wisdom: Lessons from 40 Films in 7 Minutes." YouTube video, 7:01. Posted by "we were lied to," December 28, 2012. https://www.youtube.com/watch?v=G2wIuTdf5FQ.

Rilke, Rainer Maria. *Letters to a Young Poet.* Edited by Charlie Louth. New York: Penguin Books, 2013.

Roberts, Laura Morgan, Gretchen Spreitzer, Jane Dutton, Robert Quinn, Emily Heaphy, and Barker, Brianna. "How to Play to Your Strengths." *Harvard Business Review* 83, no. 1 (2005): 74.

Russo, J. Edward and Paul Shoemaker. *Winning Decisions.* New York: Currency Books, 2002.

Saint-Exupéry, Antoine de. *The Little Prince.* New York: Harcourt, Brace & World, 1943.

Shakespeare, William. *Henry V.* Edited by Gary Taylor. Oxford: Oxford University Press, 2008.

Sinhababu, Supriya. "Full J. Z. Smith Interview." *Chicago Maroon,* June 2, 2008. http://chicagomaroon.com/2008/06/02/full-j-z-smith-interview/.

Sophocles. *The Complete Greek Tragedies: Oedipus the King, Oedipus at Colonus, Antigone.* Edited and translated by Mark Griffith, Glenn W. Most, David Grene, and Richmond Lattimore. Chicago: University of Chicago Press, 1991.

Springsteen, Bruce. *Youngstown.* Columbia Records, 1995.

Sutton, Bob. "The Dark Side of Scaling Up: Will You Want to Live in What You Build?" *Work Matters* (blog). February 12, 2015. http://bobsutton.typepad.com/.

———. "Leadership vs. Management: An Accurate but Dangerous Distinction?"

———. *Work Matters* (blog). September 11, 2008. http://bobsutton.typepad.com/.

Taxi. Directed by Tim Story. New York: 20th Century Fox, 2004. DVD.

Temple Grandin. Directed by Mick Jackson. New York: HBO Films, 2010. DVD.

Thaler, Richard H. *Misbehaving: The Making of Behavioral Economics*. New York: W. W. Norton & Co., 2015.

Thaler, Richard H., and Cass R. Sunstein. *Nudge: Improving Decisions about Health, Wealth, and Happiness*. New Haven: Yale University Press, 2008.

Wheelan, Charles. *10 1/2 Things No Commencement Speaker Has Ever Said*. New York: Norton, 2012.

Wrapp, H. Edward. "Good Managers Don't Make Policy Decisions." *Chicago Booth Selected Papers Series* 26 (1967). https://www.ChicagoBooth.edu/faculty/selected-paper-series.

INDEX

Bold numbers indicate tables; *italics* numbers indicate figures.

A

action, knowledge and, 188
action skills, 113, 188
active engagement, 39–40
active listening, 145–46
activities
    Analyzing Impact 103
    Best Advice, The 90–91
    Capital L Leadership Story, 33
    Current Definition of Leadership, 141
    Exit Ticket, 124
    Final Paper, 140
    First-Draft Leadership Definition, 43
    "I have not walked alone" Framework, 85–87
    Juxtaposing Leadership and Management, 28
    Lifelines, Past and Future Selves, 98
    Point of View, 136–37
    Strengths Data, 118–20
    This I Believe, xviii, 50–52, 62
    Vicarious Learning Framework, 71–72, 115
    Your "Top 10" Framework, 76
    Your Commencement Speech, xviii–xix, 63–64

Your Earliest Leadership Story, 13, 47–48, 95

Your Most Recent Leadership Experience, 94–95

Zero-Draft Leadership Definition, 25

adult learners, xx–xxi

adult learning theory, xx

advice, 88–92

Agnew, Mark, 128

Alchemist, The (Coelho), xvi, 78

Ali, a Life (Eig), 87

Alinsky, Saul D., 46, 47, 113

All I Did Was Ask: Conversations with Writers, Actors, Musicians, and Artists (Gross), 87

Allison, Jay, 49

Ambiguities of Experience, The (March), 161

ambiguity, managing, 73, 171, 175, 195

Ammons, A. R., 115

Anderson, Chris, 75

Apollo 13 (dir. Howard), 79, 176

Aristotle, 97

Art of Teaching Reading, The (Calkins), 138

assumptions, shedding. *See* skyscrapers, building of

availability bias, 56–57, 110–11, 147

Avasarala, Ashwin, xvii

Average Leadership Capacity, *126*

awareness, vs. understanding, 180

B

Badaracco, Joseph L., Jr., 78, 96, 104

Balis, Tony, 63

Barker, Brianna, 117–18

BATNA (Best Alternative to a Negotiated Agreement), 122

Bazerman, Max, 112

Becker, Gary S., 7

beginnings, importance of, 111, 147

behavior, 185
    components of, 156
    equation for, 24–25
    knowledge and, 113
    leadership as, 132
    personality and, 129
    situations related to, 38–39, 156–57

beliefs, 48–53

Bellow, Saul, 111

Bennington, Char, xii–xii

Bennis, Warren G., 44, 96–97, 111, 136

Bentley, Marjorie, xii, xii–xiv

Best Alternative to a Negotiated Agreement, 122

Be Wiser, Younger, *127*

biases, 21, 43, 56–57, 61, 62, 110, 147, 192

book clubs, xvii

born leaders, 126–27

Bradbury, Ray, 103

brute force approach, 186

Burnham, Daniel, 65

Burnham and Root, 65–66

Burns, James MacGregor, 25, 159

C

Calkins, Lucy, 138

Carlin, John, 81

Cattell, Raymond B., 19–20

Chaleff, Ira, 18, 39

challenge, courage and, 39

champions, 2, 154, 155
    behaviors of, 24, 39
    bringing people to the mezzanine, 60
    characteristics of, 21
    choice and, 3–4
    risk-taking and, 41

change
    self-perception of, 167
    stages of, 37–39
charisma, 36
Chicago, architecture in, 65–66
Chicago Cubs, 53–54
Chicago Tribune, 48
children, leadership book for. See *Leadership Is . . .*
choice architects, 157, 193
choices
    champions and, 3–4
    perception as, 55
    reasons for, 1
    transformation resulting from, 1–2
Coehlo, Paulo, 31, 78
coercive power, 32, 58, 163, 183
cognitive dissonance, 16
Collins, Phil, 52
commencement speeches, 62–63, 65, 169
communication, xxii, 56–57
    as leadership skill, 52
    understanding and, 60
community building, 146–48
compass, as symbol for leadership, 162
competing, 187
compliance, managing through, 58
compromising, 187
conceptual knowledge, 113, 188
confidence, building of, xvi–xvii
confirmation bias, 61, 183-86
core principles, 62
core strengths, 68
counting Fs, 110, 112, 180–84
courage, 60
    challenges and, 39
    as skill, 16–19

Covey, Stephen, 99
Crimes and Misdemeanors (dir. Allen), 132
critical thinking, 39–40
cross-functional groups, xiii
crucibles, 97
Cusack, John, 99

D
Danes, Claire, 83
data
    collecting, 114–15, 117, 187–88, 192
    as feedback, 187
    importance of, 15
    imposing order on, 73, 74
    learning from, 90
    organizing, 172
    on strengths, 118–19
Davis, Harry, 78, 113, 140, 188
Dead Poets Society (dir. Weir), 35
default mode, operating in, 2
defaults, 37, 61, 110–14, 148, 188, 192
definitions, forming for oneself, 3
Deliberative Leadership classes, xiv–xv
descriptive data, 15
development needs, 118
Dewey, John, 68, 118
domain knowledge, 113, 188
Dong, Yiqing (Liz), xvii
Drucker, Peter, 116–17, 30, 118, 154, 156, 159, 188
Dutton, Jane, 117–18

E
early leadership, 12–15, 21–23, 35, 59
early leadership experiences, 2, 95–96, 102, 115–16, 152–54
Effective Executive, The (Drucker), 116–17
Effective Followers, *40*

Eig, Jonathan, 87, **88**
Emerging Rural Leaders program (University of Chicago), xiii–xiv
Encyclopedia of Leadership (ed. Goethals, Sorenson, and Burns), 159
end-of-history illusion, 167
endings, importance of, 111, 147
Epley, Nicholas, 134
ethnocentrism, 61
executives, 147, 148
exit ticket, 189–90
experience
    as dear teacher, xix, 4, 113, 147, 187–88
    difficulties in learning from, 159
    importance of, 46–47
    learning from, 47, 70, 111, 113
    learning from one's own, 70, 94
    learning from others', 70
    organizing data from, 114–15, 122, 128
    reflecting on, 118
    as vicarious learning, 70
expert power, 36, 60, 163, 183
exploitation, 161
exploration, 161

F
Fahrenheit 451 (Bradbury), 103
Failing Forward (Maxwell), 53
Faith Church (Indiana/Illinois), xx
Fama, Eugene, 89–90
fiction, learning about leadership from, 78
followers, 39, 60
followership (following), 39–42, 164–65
    dimensions of, 39
    as form of leadership, 165
    models of, 18, 39

frameworks, 94
    creating one's own, 171–74
    creating and organizing, 70–75, 189
    for leadership development and the movies, 138–39
    reviewing, 103
    for turning off defaults, 113
Franklin, Benjamin, 4, 113, 117, 146, 187, 189, 197
Fresh Air (NPR), 87
frontiers, 187
future self, psychology of, 167–68

G
Gardner, John, 41
Garg, Sonny, 77–78
gender, leadership mythology and, 130–31
George, Bill, 136
Gilbert, Daniel, 75, 167
Ginzel frontier, 187
Giovanni, Nikki, 112
gist, 43, 46–47, 172
    communicating, 52, 56–59
    finding one's own, 47
    getting to, 52
    meaning and, 54–55
    using to manage ambiguity, 175
goals, 47
Gorman Junior High School (Colorado Springs, CO), 14–15
Gosling, Jonathan, 135
green pens, 121–23
Gross, Terry, 87
group experiences, 5
groupthink, 61

H

Haas, Howard, 6, 78
habits, 2, 97, 110
Hagiya, Grant, 106
happenings, turning into experiences, 114, 139
happiness, 75
Harris, Katie, 12
Hass, Howard, 58
Heaphy, Emily, 117–18
Hellman, Todd, 124
helping, in leadership role, 105
Hemingway, Ernest, 135, 194
Henderson, Bill, xii, xiv–xv
Henley, William Ernest, 82–83
Henry V (Shakespeare), 78
hero worship, 100
Hesse, Hermann, 78
heuristics, 110, 197
High Fidelity (dir. Frears), 99
high school, 14, 15–16
    athletics in, xv–xvii
    leadership curriculum for, xiii–xviii
hindsight bias, 111, 182
Hogarth, Robin, 34, 113, 148, 188
Holmes, Oliver Wendell, Jr., 77
hope, 54
human capital, 7

I

ideas
    needing champions, 23
    salience of, 149
identity
    changing, through behavioral change, 168–69
    linked to outcomes, 16–17
Immelt, Jeff, 56

Inception (dir. Nolan), 100
influences, identifying, 97–98
insight skills, 113, 115
internal framework, strengthening, 65–68
interviewing, learning through, 87–88
Inui, Edny, 74
"Invictus" (Henley), 82–83
Invictus (dir. Eastwood), 79, 81–83, 176

J

Jacobs, Don, 34
Jenney, William Le Baron, 66–68
Jobs, Steve, 4
Johnson, Benjamin, 53–54
Jonathan Eig's Interview Advice, **88**
Jones, Ned, 89
Joubert, Joseph, 105
Journey to the East, The (Hesse), 78
Jurasius, Beck, xii, xv–xvii

K

Kalanithi, Paul, 99–100
Kass, Miriam, 138
Kellerman, Barbara, 39
Kelley, Robert, 39
Kennedy, John F., 141
King, Martin Luther, Jr., 36, 77
King Lear (Shakespeare), 78
knowledge
    action and, 181
    application of, 60–61
    vs. wisdom, 46–47
Konnikova, Maria, 134
Korsombut, Akkaravuth (March), xvii
Kotter, John, 2
Kwoing, Jasmine, xii, xvii

L

labels

    importance of, 155–56, 162

    leadership and, 156

    unfreezing, 158

Laozi, 21

Larrick, Richard, 4, 132

Last Lecture, The (Pausch), 100

leaders, 154–55

    stereotypes about, 155, 193

leadership (leading), 6, 15, 158

    acknowledgment of, 15–16

    as action rather than label, 20

    affecting others through, 100–103

    athletics and, xvi–xvii

    as behavior, xii, 21, 24, 132, 155, 191

    as behavior of champions, 39

    with capital L or lowercase l, 156

    as choice, 1, 3, 24–25, 55–56, 65, 151, 162

    changing the conversation about, 19–20

    compasses and, 36–37

    curiosity and, 48

    customizing learning for, 47

    danger of, 58

    defining, xii, 3, 12, 43, 141, 145, 151, 158–60, 164

    early experiences in, 2, 95–96, 102, 115–16, 151–53

    faith in, 41

    framework for, 7

    gist (essence) of, 43

    as helping role, 100–105

    human process of, 92

    as industry, 6–7

    as journey into self, 56

    labels and, 20, 21, 155

    vs. management, xix, 2–3, 4, 47, 55–56, 132, 161

    multidisciplinary nature of, 6

    myths about, 129–32, 134, 155. *See also* leadership: stereotypes about

    needing followers' heads and hearts, 35, 164

    parallels of, with architecture, 65–68

    personality-based view of, 193

    point of view about, 136–38

    questions for, 104–7

    relationship building and, 22–23

    role models for, 100–103

    of self, 1–2

    as skill, 7

    stereotypes and, 37–38, 43. *See also* leadership: myths about

    traits of, 19–21, 36, 39

    understanding, 46–47

    values related to, 18

    as verb, 20, 24–25, 58, 132, 154–55, 156, 159, 191–92

    vision and, 16

    words associated with, 28–31

Leadership BS (Pfeffer), 6–7

leadership capacity

    average, 126–27

    enhancing, 127–28

leadership capital, 7, 145, 158

leadership development

    activities for, sources for, 138–39

    curriculum for, xiii–xvii

    industry for, xxii–xxiii, 145

    self-examination and, 4

Leadership Is . . . (Ginzel), 31

Leadership and Management, **29**

Leadership Modules, 5
    Beginnings and Endings, 147–48
    Best Advice, 180
    Be Wiser, Younger, 191–92
    Building Community, 145–47
    Choosing Leadership Introduction, 148–50
    Counting Fs, 183–87
    Definition of Success, 167–68
    Early Leadership Story, 151–54
    Exit Ticket, 189
    First Follower, The, 164–65
    Focus on Strengths, 188–89
    Juxtapositions, 161–62
    Labels, 154–56
    Leadership at the Movies, 176–81
    Leadership Myth Busting, 193–94
    Life Lessons, 181–82
    Map and Compass, The, 162–64
    Public Lectures and Speeches, 175
    Recent Leadership Story, 181–82
    Structural Integrity, 169–70
    Think Like a Social Psychologist, 156–57
    This I Believe, 167
    Vicarious Learning, 171–75
    Zeigarnik Effect, The, 194–95
    Zero-Draft Leadership Definition, 194–95
leadership stories
    Connie's, 17–18, 59–60
    Daniel's, 102
    Henry's, 115–16
    Ivan's, 1–2
    Jake's, 35
    Jennifer's, 130–32
    Joe's, 100–101
    Laura's, 48–49
    Lena's, 40–41
    Sel's, 18–19
    Shilpa's, 21–23
Leading for a Lifetime (Bennis and Thomas), 97
Leavitt, Harold, 24, 32, 43, 62
legitimate power, 32, 58, 60, 163, 183–84
"Letter from Birmingham Jail" (King), 77
Letterman, David, 75, 175
Lewin, Kurt, xxiii, 24–25, 37–38, 128, 129, 156, 172
Lewis, Randy, 39, 83, 105
life story, summarizing by events, 99
literature, importance of reading, 78, 82
Little Prince, The (Saint-Exupéry), xv–xvi
Lovell, James, 79

M
management (managing)
    as behavior, 155, 191
    as behavior of champions, 39
    as choice, 24–25
    being in the present, 162
    vs. leadership, 2–3, 31, 47
    leading and, xix, 4, 55–56
    maps and, 36–37
    needing followers' heads, 35
    nobility of, 32
    power and, 32
    present activity of, 36–37
    putting on same plane as leadership, 161
    social psychology and, 5
    stereotypes and, 37
    as verb, 20, 24–25, 58, 132, 154–55, 161, 191–92
    words associated with, 28–31
manager, label of, 21
manager-leader, 43, 62
managers, 154–55

characteristics associated with, 20–21
    stereotypes around, 155
Mandela, Nelson, 81, 176
map, as symbol for the present, 163
March, James, 139, 161
marriage, change and, 38
Maxwell, John C., 53
McGregor, Douglas, 30
McNulty, Eric, 52
Meadow, Scott, 92
meaning, management of, 56–58
mezzanine, 172
    as place for communicating gist, 59–62
    communicating on, 172–73
middle children, 155
Mindwise (Epley), 134
Minow, Nell, 79
Minsky, Marvin, 41, 159, 193
Mintzberg, Henry, 135
Misbehaving (Thaler), 7, 191–92
modeling, 70, 100–103
Monadnock Building (Chicago), 65–66
moral action, 18
motivations, understanding, 56, 107
movement, creating, 165
Movie Mom's Guide to Family Movies, The (Minow), 79
movies, learning about leadership from, 78–85, 99, 138–39, 176–77. *See also individual movie titles*
Myers-Briggs type indicator, 129
myths, about leadership, 129–32, 134

N
negative role models, 100–101
negotiation skills, 188
Neruda, Pablo, 122
normal neurotics, 61, 110, 111, 184

Northwestern University, Kellogg School of Management, 34
noticers, first-class, 111–12
Nudge (Thaler and Sunstein), 61–62

O
obituary, writing one's own, 99
observation, importance of, 123
On Becoming a Leader (Bennis), 96–97, 136
opt-in programs, automatic, 61–62
Othello (Shakespeare), 78
overconfidence bias, 111, 184

P
Pandji, Grace Soetikno, xxii–xxiii
parenting, as leadership role, 17–18
Pareto frontier, 187
participant-observation, 123
Passy, Barbara, 19
Pausch, Randy, 100
peer discussions, 5
perception, as choice, 55
performance reviews, 111, 118
personal development, 70
personal frameworks, 67–68
personality, behavior and, 129
personality psychology, 157
personality tests, 20
"Personal Manifesto, The" (McNulty), 52
personal strategy, 140–41
Pfeffer, Jeff, 6–7, 56, 88–89
Phelps, Michael, xv
Picasso, Pablo, 104
Playing the Enemy (Carlin), 81
poetry, learning from, 82–83

point of view
    developing, 136–38, 159
    IQ and, 159, 193
power
    leadership and, 36
    types of, 32, 36, 180–81. *See also* coercive power; expert power; legitimate power; referent power; reward power
Power of Noticing, The (Bazerman), 112
pre-hire testing, 20
Preparation Worksheet [for role-playing], **121**
present, staying in, 146
primacy effect, 111
Principles of Topological Psychology (Lewin), 24
prison, recidivism and, 38
professional strategy, 140–41
project teams, 48–49
punctuation points, 96–98

Q

Quinn, Robert, 117–18

R

racism, resistance to, 19
Rashomon (dir. Kurosawa), 79–80, 176
RBS. *See* Reflected Best Self
recency bias, 148
recency effect, 111
Reel Wisdom (YouTube video), 176–79
referent power, 36, 164, 183
Reflected Best Self, 118
refreezing, 37–38
Reiser, Kimberly, xii, xviii–xix
relationships, building of, and leadership, 22–23

responsibility
    assuming, 18
    sense of, 60
reversible figures, 54–55, 151
reward power, 32, 58, 163, 183
Riddering, Rick, xii, xx–xxi
Rilke, Rainer Maria, 105
risk-taking, 41
Roberts, Harry, 89–90
Roberts, Laura Morgan, 117–18
role models, 100–103
role-playing, 121–22
Roosevelt, Eleanor, 36
Root, John, 65
Russo, J. Edward, 115

S

safety, as concern, 59–60
Samuelson, Paul A., 105
Schoemaker, Paul J. H., 115
segregation, fighting against, 18–19
self
    finding one's own gist, 47
    leadership of, 1–2
    leadership as journey into, 56
    as work in progress, 1
self-esteem, biases and, 110, 111
self-reflection, 96–97
self-to-text/film connections, 138
self-understanding (self-awareness; self-discovery), xvi, 4, 13, 15, 47, 52–53, 56
    embracing, 139
    leadership and, 20
    questions for, 106–8
7 Habits of Highly Effective People, The (Covey), 99
Shakespeare, William, 78
Shim, Joon, xii, xxi–xxii

shortcuts, 110, 192

situations, behavior related to, 25, 38–39

skills, practicing, 16

skyscrapers, building of, 65–68, 169

Smith, Jonathan Z., 135

social psychology, 5, 16, 24–25, 38–39, 97, 110, 128, 132–34, 147, 148, 156–57, 168. 172, 185, 188, 193

Socratic method, 48

Soetikno, Grace, xii

Sophocles, 78, 117

SPA Vicarious-Learning Framework, **74**

Spreitzer, Gretchen, 117–18

Springsteen, Bruce, 77

Star Wars, 194

staying in the question, 134–35

stereotypes, 156

strengths, focusing on, 115–20, 188–89

strong situations, 132–34, 157–58

structural integrity, 164, 169

Stumbling on Happiness (Gilbert), 75

success, 52, 167–69

Sun, Wilson, xvii

Sunstein, Cass, 61

surgical training, xxi–xxii

Sutton, Bob, 28, 136

symbols, 56–58, 121

T

task completion, 134–35

Taxi (dir. Story), 117

TED Talks, 75, 85

Temple Grandin (dir. Jackson), 79, 83–85, 176

tendencies, 147

10 1/2 Things No Commencement Speaker Has Ever Said (Wheelan), 63

text-to-film connections, 138

text-to-text connections, 138

Thaler, Richard, 7, 61, 154, 157, 191, 193

This I Believe (NPR), 50, 85

Thomas, Robert J., 97

Thoreau, Henry David, 179

360-feedback review, 118

"Three Questions, The" (Tolstoy), 105

TKI. *See* Thomas-Kilmann Instrument

Tolstoy, Leo, 105

top-10 lists, 75–77, 88, 175–76

transformation, leadership and, 33

Trinity Christian College, xx

Twain, Mark, 192

U

understanding

    vs. awareness, 180

    as leadership skill, 52

    levels of, 60–61

    turning into experiences, 46, 96, 191

unfreezing, 37–38

University of Chicago

    Booth School of Business, xi, xii–xiii, 34

    Emerging Rural Leaders program, xiii–xiv

V

values, 18, 47, 48, 57

Values in Action (VIA) Character Strengths Profile, 189

vicarious learning, 70–71, 171–75

vicarious-learning framework, 115

videos

    Behavior, 156

    Earliest Leadership Experience, 151–52

    First Follower, The, 164

    Focus on Strengths, 188–89

    Ginzel Frontier, The, 187

    How Labels Manage Meaning, 154–55

Introduction to *Choosing Leadership*, 148–49

Join Me on the Mezzanine, 172–73

Map and the Compass, The, 162–63

Psychology of Future Self, The, 167

Reel Wisdom, 176–77

Surprising Science of Happiness, The, 175

What's Your Definition of Leadership?, 158–59

What's Your Definition of Success?, 168–69

vision

    coming from understanding the present, 162, 163

    leadership and, 30

volunteering, 14–15

volunteer student council, 14–15, 152

W

Walgreens, 105

Way I See It, The: A Personal Look at Autism and Asperger's (Grandin), 85

Weick, Karl, 37

Wheelan, Charles, 63

When Breath Becomes Air (Kalanithi), 99–100

Winning Decisions (Russo and Schoemaker), 115

wisdom

    gaining of, xix, 3

    vs. knowledge, 46–47

Wrapp, Ed, 106

writing, importance of, xix, 5, 7, 44, 114–15, 140, 154,179–180, 192

Z

Zaleznik, Abraham, 39

Zeigarnik, Bluma, 134–35

Zeigarnik effect, 134–36, 194–95

zero draft, 71, 159–60

zigzag bridge, 57

ABOUT THE AUTHOR

Photo credit: Tomer Keysar

LINDA GINZEL, PHD, is a clinical professor of managerial psychology at the University of Chicago's Booth School of Business and the founder of its customized executive education program. For over three decades, she has developed and taught MBA and executive education courses in negotiation, leadership capital, managerial psychology, and more. Linda has also taught MBA and PhD students at Northwestern and Stanford, as well as designed customized educational programs for many Fortune 500 companies. She has received numerous teaching awards for excellence in MBA education, as well as the President's Service Award for her work with the nonprofit Kids In Danger. Linda lives in Chicago with her husband. She is Korean American.